An American in Britain

The Essential Guide for Stress-Free Travel in the UK

S. J. Thomas

Sweet Harmony Press

Paperback ISBN: 978-1-948713-50-4
eBook ISBN: 978-1-948713-51-1
Audiobook ISBN: 978-1-948713-52-8

© Copyright 2025 by S.J. Thomas and Sweet Harmony Press - All rights reserved.

The content contained within this book may not be reproduced, duplicated, or transmitted without direct written permission from the author or the publisher.

Under no circumstances will any blame or legal responsibility be held against the publisher or author for any damages, reparation, or monetary loss due to the information contained within this book, either directly or indirectly.

Legal Notice:

This book is copyright protected. It is only for personal use. You cannot amend, distribute, sell, use, quote or paraphrase any part, or the content within this book, without the consent of the author or publisher.

Disclaimer Notice:

Please note the information contained within this document is for educational and entertainment purposes only. All effort has been executed to present accurate, up to date, reliable, complete information. No warranties of any kind are declared or implied. Readers acknowledge that the author is not engaged in the rendering of legal, financial, medical or professional advice. The content within this book has been derived from various sources. Please consult a licensed professional before attempting any techniques outlined in this book.

By reading this document, the reader agrees that under no circumstances is the author responsible for any losses, direct or indirect, that are incurred as a result of the use of the information contained within this document, including, but not limited to, errors, omissions, or inaccuracies.

For bulk orders, contact info@sweetharmonypress.com

For more info visit www.anamericaninbritain.com

Contents

Preface	IV
1. Preparing for Your Journey	1
2. Navigating British Transportation	7
3. All Aboard! UK Train Travel	18
4. Driving in the UK	34
5. Money Matters	43
6. Communication and Connectivity	49
7. Electrical Appliances and Connectivity	56
8. Where to Stay?	60
9. Eating Out and British Cuisine	69
10. At the Grocery Store	78
11. Shopping in the UK	83
12. Health and Medical Care	88
13. I Love It Here! Moving to the UK	96
14. Conclusion and Travel Tips	102
15. Appendix	106
16. References	109

Preface

Welcome to *An American in Britain*!

Congratulations on planning your trip to the United Kingdom, a destination brimming with history, culture, and unique charm. Whether you're excited to explore London's iconic landmarks, wander through quaint countryside villages, or simply enjoy the food, shopping, and traditions, this guide is here to ensure your experience is as seamless and enjoyable as possible.

Traveling to a new country, especially one that feels familiar yet so different, can come with its challenges. But don't worry! This guide is designed to help you navigate every practical aspect of your trip. From figuring out transportation options to understanding British etiquette, managing money, and even staying connected, you'll find everything you need to feel like a confident traveler.

Why This Guide?

The goal of this guide is simple: to take the guesswork out of your trip. It's written specifically for American travelers, with clear, step-by-step instructions and helpful tips that address common questions (and even a few things you might not think of!). If this is your first time visiting the UK, or you're returning for another adventure, using this insightful guide will help you make the most of your time across the pond.

How to Use This Guide

This guide is organized into easy-to-follow sections so you can quickly find the information you need. If you're in the planning stage, start with the chapters on preparing for your journey and packing. Once you're in the UK, refer to sections on transportation, dining, or managing money whenever you need quick advice.

You'll also find handy references, useful tips and important contact information in the appendices for when you're on the go. Keep this guide handy! It's your companion for all things practical while navigating the UK.

A Quick Note About UK Culture

While the UK and the US share a language and a long history, you'll notice a few differences right away. From the humor (yes, it's often dry and sarcastic!) to driving on the left side of the road, there are cultural nuances that make the UK wonderfully unique. Learning a bit about these differences before your trip will make your experience all the more rewarding, and help you avoid a few faux pas along the way!

Cultural Etiquette and Tips

- **Politeness is very important**: Brits are known for their politeness. Saying "please," "thank you," and "sorry" (even when it's not your fault!) goes a long way.

- **Queuing (lining up):** Brits love a good queue. Always wait your turn, whether it's for a bus, at a shop, or in a queue for attractions.

- **Tipping:** It's different from the US Most restaurants include a service charge, and tipping is not as common or expected.

- **Humor:** British humor can sometimes feel like a puzzle; it's often dry, subtle, and self-deprecating. Don't be afraid to laugh along!

- **Small talk:** Brits enjoy small talk, especially about the weather. It's a great way to break the ice.

- **Dates:** British dates are listed as day-month-year. For example, 01-10-2025 is actually Oct 1st 2025.

Cultural Nuances and Differences From the US

- **Driving:** The UK drives on the left side of the road, which can feel counterintuitive at first.

- **Measurements:** You'll encounter the metric system for most things, but distances on road signs are still in miles.

- **Money:** Instead of dollars and cents, you'll use pounds and pence. The coins can feel confusing at first, but don't worry, this guide includes an illustrated breakdown.

- **Food names:** Some food terms might differ—"chips" are fries, "crisps" are chips, and a "biscuit" is a cookie. Don't worry, you'll adjust quickly!

So, get to know these small but important details, and you'll not only steer clear of awkward moments but also fall in love with the unique charm of British culture. Grab a cup of tea (or coffee, if you prefer), and let's dive into all the tips and advice you need to make your UK adventure unforgettable!

Chapter One

Preparing for Your Journey

So, you're getting ready to hop across the pond—how exciting! Prepping is the first step you'll take toward having an unforgettable adventure. Don't worry, though! I've got your back. This chapter is here to make sure you've ticked all the boxes before boarding that plane.

Let's dive into passports, packing, and all the other fun stuff that will help you glide through your journey like a pro.

Essential Documents: Passport, Visa Information, and Travel Insurance

Okay, first things first: Let's talk paperwork. The absolute non-negotiable item for your trip is your passport. According to *Processing Times for US Passports* (2024), if you don't have one yet, apply ASAP, because these things can take weeks—or even months—to process. Already have a passport? High five! Just make sure it's valid for the entire time you'll be in the UK (Morris, 2023). While the UK doesn't enforce a six-month rule like some countries, do yourself a favor and check the expiration date now (seriously, go check). If it's cutting it close, renewing it before your trip is a smart move.

And while we're on the topic of things you don't want to skip: travel insurance. Yes, it's an extra expense, but trust me, it's worth it. Imagine your flight gets canceled, or your luggage decides to take a solo trip to Paris. Travel insurance has your back. Plus, it'll cover medical emergencies because (fun fact) the UK's fabulous and free National Health Service (NHS) doesn't extend its magical powers to tourists. According to the Office for Health Improvement and Disparities (2014), though the UK has a strong healthcare system, as a tourist or non-native, you may need to pay for certain services. And, more fun surprises, your US health insurance may not cover you outside of the US! Therefore, look for a policy that covers trip interruptions, health emergencies, and even evacuation (you know, just in case).

New for 2025: Electronic Travel Authorization (ETA)

Now, let's talk about a new kid on the block: the Electronic Travel Authorization (ETA). Starting in 2025, all US citizens traveling either for business purposes or tourism for up to six months will need to get this fancy little document before heading to the UK (Home Office et al., 2024). Don't worry, it's super simple. You'll fill out an online form, pay a small fee, and *voilà*—your ETA is linked to your passport. Easy-peasy. Just make sure to apply at least a few weeks before your trip to avoid any last-minute drama. Check out the latest info at https://www.gov.uk/guidance/apply-for-an-electronic-travel-authorisation-eta.

Packing for the UK: Weather Considerations and Essentials

Alright, let's tackle packing. The UK's weather is like that unpredictable friend who keeps you guessing. Sunny one moment, rainy the next, with a side of wind for good measure. The secret to surviving British weather? Layers, my friend, layers. Think t-shirts, sweaters, and a trusty waterproof jacket. You don't need to bring your entire wardrobe, just pack smart.

A word about umbrellas: Yes, the UK is famous for its rain, but here's the thing, umbrellas can be a bit of a gamble. The wind often likes to flip them inside out at the worst possible moment. If you're a fan of staying dry, a good-quality waterproof jacket with a hood is your best bet. And for shoes? Comfort is king. You'll be doing a ton of walking (cobblestones and all), so bring sturdy, weather-resistant footwear that won't leave your feet crying at the end of the day.

Let's not forget the tech! The UK uses Type G plugs, so you'll need an adapter for your chargers. And check if your devices are dual-voltage (most modern ones are, so you're probably fine). If not, you might also need a voltage converter to avoid frying your favorite gadgets.

Finally, leave a little extra room in your suitcase. Why? Because you're going to want to bring back souvenirs! Whether it's a Harry Potter scarf, some authentic shortbread, or a cute tea towel, the UK is full of goodies that you'll want to pack home.

Is The UK a Safe Place to Visit?

Yes! The United Kingdom ranks among the safest countries you'll visit. While no place is entirely crime-free, your UK adventure will likely feel remarkably secure compared to many US cities. The most significant difference you'll notice? The near-total absence of gun violence due to the UK's strict firearms legislation.

Gun Laws: A Cultural Shift

The UK has some of the world's strictest gun control laws, with handguns effectively banned and other firearms heavily regulated. Even most police officers don't routinely carry guns—instead, you'll see "unarmed officers" handling everyday policing. This fundamental difference creates a notably different atmosphere in confrontations and public spaces.

London vs. American Cities: A Safety Comparison

London, like any major global city, has its share of petty crime, but violent crime rates pale in comparison to many US metropolitan areas. The most common tourist concerns are pickpocketing in crowded areas and phone snatching (particularly around Underground stations). Unlike some American cities, you won't find "no-go zones" in London—most neighborhoods are perfectly safe to explore during daylight hours.

Urban vs. Rural Britain: Different Landscapes, Different Concerns

Rural Britain feels almost idyllically safe. Village crime typically involves agricultural issues or minor property matters rather than personal safety threats. The greatest dangers in the countryside? Narrow roads, unexpected weather changes on hikes, and perhaps an occasional territorial farm animal! Meanwhile, urban areas follow familiar patterns—be more vigilant in city centers, transport hubs, late at night and tourist hotspots.

Smart Travel Tips for American Visitors

- **Blend in**: Lower your speaking volume slightly (Americans tend to speak louder than Brits) and avoid obviously tourist-y behaviors when possible.

- **Stay alert in crowded areas**: Tourist hotspots like Oxford Street, Camden Market, and major attractions are prime territory for pickpockets.

- **Secure your belongings**: Consider cross-body bags with zippers and keep your phone secure, especially when near street entrances on the Tube.

- **Emergency number**: Remember to dial 999 (not 911) for emergencies.

- **Night safety**: Use well-lit, busy streets when walking after dark, and consider using ride-sharing apps for late-night journeys.

- **Traffic awareness**: Always look right first when crossing roads—this unfamiliar pattern causes many tourist accidents!

The UK offers a wonderfully safe travel experience that lets you focus on making memories rather than worrying about security. With these basic precautions in mind, you're all set to explore this fascinating country with confidence and peace of mind!

Understanding UK Geography and Regions

Now that your suitcase is ready, let's talk geography and take a closer look at where you're headed:

Countries That Make Up the UK

The UK isn't just one big island with a funny accent (or, to be precise, several funny accents). It's actually made up of four countries: England, Scotland, Wales, and Northern Ireland. Each has its own culture, traditions, and even its own national dish (hello, haggis and Welsh cakes!).

- England is the biggest and home to London, the sprawling, history-packed capital. But it's not all city life. You'll find rolling countryside, charming villages, and famous landmarks like Stonehenge and the Cotswolds.

- Scotland is where you'll find bagpipes, kilts, and some of the most jaw-dropping landscapes on the planet. Think rugged Highlands, serene lochs, and castles galore. Don't forget Edinburgh, with its world-famous festivals and old-world charm.

- Wales is all about castles, coastal beauty, and a language that looks like someone threw Scrabble tiles at the wall (it's Welsh, and yes, it's fascinating). Cardiff is its vibrant capital.

- Northern Ireland offers a mix of stunning landscapes like the Giant's Causeway and a rich history you can explore in Belfast. It's small but mighty, with some of the friendliest people you'll ever meet.

The UK vs. Britain vs. the British Isles

Now, here's a fun fact to impress your friends: "The UK," "Great Britain", and "The British Isles" are *not* the same thing. **The United Kingdom (UK)** includes England, Scotland, Wales, and Northern Ireland. **Great Britain**, on the other hand, refers to just England, Scotland, and Wales—it's the big island. And **the British Isles**? That's a geographical term that includes all the islands in the area, including Ireland, which is its own independent country. (*The Difference Between the UK, Great Britain and the British Isles, 2011*)

However, you will find in this book, I tend to use "The UK" and "Britain" pretty interchangeably. Sorry about that Northern Ireland.

Overview of County Names and Regional Names

In addition to its countries, the UK is divided into counties, which are similar to states in the US. For example, Cornwall in the southwest is famous for its beaches and pasties, Yorkshire in the north is known for its rolling hills, sheep and cheese, and Kent in the southeast is often called the "Garden of England" for its lush landscapes.

Counties are also grouped into larger regions, such as the North West, the Midlands, and the South East, which are often referenced in weather reports or travel guides (Kellner & Thomas, 2025).

Review of Major Cities

Speaking of cities, London is, of course, the UK's bustling capital and the starting point for many visitors. Beyond London, there are plenty of vibrant cities worth exploring. Edinburgh, Scotland's historic capital, is known for its festivals and iconic castles. Manchester, a hub of music and culture, is a must-visit for sports fans and concert-goers alike. In Wales, Cardiff combines modern waterfront attractions with medieval history. Belfast, in Northern Ireland, offers a mix of history, culture, and stunning coastal scenery. Each city has its unique vibe, so don't be afraid to venture beyond the capital.

So, there you have it: your first steps toward a fabulous UK adventure. With your documents sorted, your suitcase packed, and your newfound geography knowledge, you're officially ready to conquer the UK. Go ahead and sip tea in a London café, hike the Scottish Highlands, or wander through a Welsh castle – you'll be glad you took the time to prep like a pro.

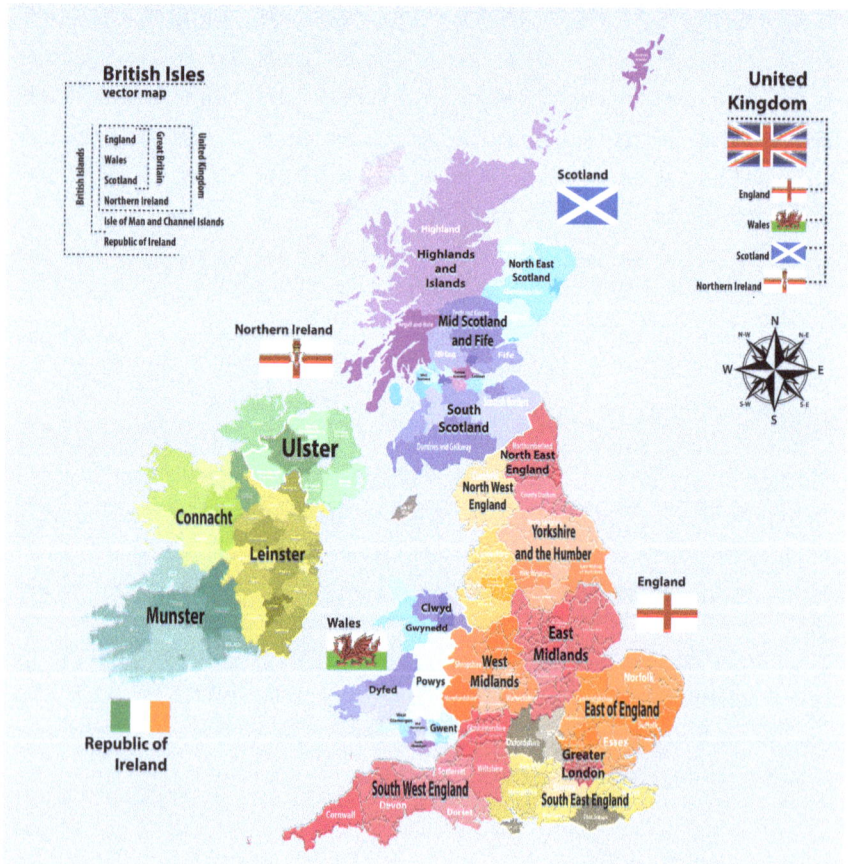

Map of the British Isles

Chapter Two

Navigating British Transportation

Welcome to one of the most exciting parts of your UK adventure: getting around! Now, I know what you're thinking—transportation doesn't exactly scream "fun." But trust me, navigating Britain's buses, trains, taxis, and tubes can be an adventure in itself! The UK has one of the most efficient and well-connected transport systems in the world, and once you get the hang of it, you'll be whizzing around like a local.

Ready to hit the road (or the tracks)? Let's go!

Navigating Airports and Airport Transfers

If you're flying into the UK, you'll likely land at one of its major airports, like Heathrow, Gatwick, or Manchester. These airports are massive, but they're also well-organized, with clear signs to help you find your way. However, the UK's airports aren't just for arrivals—they're also excellent jumping-off points for exploring further afield, both within the UK and beyond.

The London area alone has six airports:

- **London Heathrow (LHR):** A huge, bustling airport and the main hub for most US inbound flights.

- **London Gatwick (LGW):** London's second-busiest airport, located 28 miles south of the city, known for European leisure routes and long-haul flights to Asia and the Americas.

- **London City Airport (LCY):** Convenient for central London and business travelers.

- **London Luton (LTN), London Stansted (STN), and London

Southend (SEN): Smaller airports, perfect for budget airlines and short-haul flights to Europe.

If you're considering a hop to destinations like Edinburgh, Belfast, or even a European getaway, these smaller airports can be a fantastic alternative to the mega-hub of Heathrow.

Other Airports in the British Isles:

- **Edinburgh Airport (EDI):** Scotland's busiest airport, with excellent European and domestic connections just 8 miles from the city.
- **Manchester Airport (MAN):** The UK's third-largest airport with three terminals and extensive long-haul routes to Asia and North America.
- **Belfast International Airport (BFS):** Northern Ireland's main airport, focusing on UK domestic flights and European holiday destinations.
- **Dublin Airport (DUB):** Ireland's largest airport with US preclearance facilities and extensive transatlantic routes.

Of course, landing in London is not your only option. Sometimes it is much cheaper to get a flight to somewhere in Europe, and then catch a connecting flight to one of the London airports on one of the budget airlines like EasyJet.

Arrivals at London Heathrow (LHR)

Since most passengers do arrive to the UK via LHR, let's walk through navigating one of the world's busiest airports like a seasoned traveler.

First things first - Heathrow is massive, and those walks from the gate can feel like a mini-marathon after a long flight! The journey from your arrival gate to immigration can take up to 20 minutes, sometimes even longer. If you or anyone in your party might struggle with the distance, don't hesitate to arrange assistance in advance through your airline. They'll have a wheelchair or open cart ready to whisk you through those seemingly endless corridors!

Now, here's some great news for eligible travelers: those automatic eGates at immigration can be your fast track to London! If you're 12 or older and carrying a

US passport with a chip (look for the small camera icon on the cover), you can skip the regular lines and use these digital gates. Just remove your glasses, any hats, and look straight at the camera - it's like taking a high-tech selfie! The whole process usually takes less than a minute, compared to potentially long waits in the staffed lines.

<u>Pro tip</u>: While you're making that long walk from the gate, use the time to have your passport ready and take a quick look at the screens directing you to either the eGates or regular immigration lines. And if you're arriving early morning (between 6-9 AM), brace yourself for the busiest immigration times when multiple long-haul flights arrive simultaneously. You might want to make a quick stop into the restroom (called "toilets" or "the loo" in the UK), as you never know how long the line at the eGates might be.

After clearing immigration, follow the signs to baggage reclaim (that's British for baggage claim). While you're waiting for your bags, look for the free luggage trolleys - they're a blessing after that long walk through the terminal. Each baggage hall has screens showing which carousel your flight's bags will appear on, and you'll usually find your airline's logo displayed above the correct belt. Once you have all your luggage, follow the signs for taxis or the express train.

Where To Next?

Getting from the airport to your destination is a breeze. Most airports have express trains (like the Heathrow Express or the Gatwick Express) that will zip you into the city center in under 30 minutes. Regional airports often have convenient rail and bus connections as well.

Heading into London from Heathrow? Consider zooming in on the Heathrow Express! This sleek train service is basically your fast track into the heart of London, bringing you from the airport to Paddington Station in just 15 minutes (seriously, it's that quick!). The trains are super comfortable with plenty of space for your luggage, great WiFi (because we know you'll want to post those "Just landed!" photos), and they run every 15 minutes. Pro tip: book your tickets online before you fly - you'll save a good chunk of change compared to buying them at the station. Once you reach Paddington, you can easily hop on the Underground or grab a taxi to your final destination. Oh, and don't worry about getting lost in the airport - just follow the clearly marked signs with the train symbol, and you'll spot the Heathrow Express stations in Terminals 2, 3, and 5. If you're landing at Terminal 4, there's a free transfer service to get you to the main train. Trust me, after a long flight, there's nothing better than knowing you'll be in central London before your jet lag even kicks in!

Pro tip: For any airport arrival, book your airport transfer (whether it's a train, bus, taxi or private car hire) in advance if you can. It's one less thing to worry about after a long flight, especially during peak travel times. When you have booked a private car, the driver will be in the Arrivals hall holding a sign with your name. Also be sure to have the number of the company you booked handy, just in case you can't find your driver (there are dozens of drivers waiting for passengers, especially in the 6-9 morning hours). Be extra sure you are connected with the right driver and company.

Important Safety tip: If anyone approaches you in the airport arrival hall (or at any station) offering a taxi ride, just smile and keep walking. These unofficial drivers might seem friendly, but they're actually not licensed or regulated - definitely not what you want for your first ride in London! Instead, either head to the official taxi rank (just follow the signs with the black cab symbol) where you'll find London's famous black cabs waiting, or use your pre-booked car service or ride-sharing app. The official taxi rank is right outside each terminal, and the pick-up points for pre-booked services are clearly marked. Trust me, starting your London adventure safely is totally worth taking these few extra steps!

Overview of Public Transportation in the UK

Public transportation is the backbone of travel in the UK, and you'll quickly find that it's efficient, affordable (well, mostly), and incredibly easy to use. From iconic red double-decker buses to sleek trains that zip between cities, you'll have plenty of options to choose from. For American visitors, the extent of public transport options might feel a little overwhelming at first, but rest assured, it's easy to navigate once you know the basics.

In the UK, you'll find a combination of buses, trains, trams, and underground systems (like London's famous Tube). Unlike the US, where cars dominate, public transportation is often the easiest and cheapest way to get around (Collins, 2024). In cities like London, Edinburgh, and Manchester, buses and trains run constantly, making it easy to get from Point A to Point B. In smaller towns and rural areas, you'll still find buses and trains, but they might not run as frequently, so it's always a good idea to check schedules in advance (Cowie, 2017).

To help you navigate routes and timetables, and make your journey smoother, download these transportation must-have apps:

- **Citymapper:** Perfect for navigating cities like London, Manchester, or Birmingham. It covers buses, trains, and even walking routes.

- **National Rail:** The go-to app for checking train schedules and buying tickets.

- **Trainline:** Another excellent app for booking train journeys across the UK.

Pro tip: Always check schedules in advance. While public transport is generally reliable, rural areas may have limited services, and even big cities can experience delays (hello, signal failures!).

Buses, Trains, and the Tube in Major Cities

Let's break it down by mode of transport:

Buses

The UK's buses are iconic, and they're a fantastic way to see the sights while getting around. In London, the famous red double-deckers are both functional and fun—grab a seat on the top deck for great views of the city! To make your adventures even easier, download the Bus Times App (or a similar bus app like Citymapper) before your trip. These handy apps will help you find the nearest stops, check schedules, and even track buses in real time, so you'll never be left wondering when your ride will arrive. And bus travel is a bargain – just a flat-rate standard fare, currently £1.75, no matter what distance you travel!

But London's buses aren't the only stars of the show! In other cities like Manchester, Birmingham, and Edinburgh, buses are just as convenient and easy to use. Payment is usually contactless (via a debit/credit card or phone), and fares are quite reasonable. If you're planning a longer journey, you can use coach services like National Express or Megabus, which connect cities and towns across the UK at budget-friendly prices, making it a great way to travel further afield without breaking the bank.

Trains

The UK's train network is extensive and connects major cities, towns, and even the countryside. Trains are fast, comfortable, and often scenic (especially in Scotland or the Lake District) and you can travel between cities like London, Edinburgh, and Cardiff in just a few hours (Cowie, 2017). This topic is so important, we have dedicated the entire next chapter just for train travel.

The Tube

If you're in London, the Tube (also known as the London Underground) will be your go-to. With 11 color-coded lines and over 270 stations, it's an impressive feat of engineering that virtually connects every corner of the city and can feel a bit overwhelming at first. But don't worry—we'll guide you on how to use it step by step.

First things first: don't be intimidated by that colorful map - it's actually super user-friendly once you get the hang of it! Each line has its own color (like the Piccadilly line is dark blue, and the Central line is red), and stations are clearly marked along each route. When you're planning your journey, look for the station name you want on the map, then trace back to where you are - the line colors will show you if you need to change trains. Most stations have giant maps on the walls, or you can grab a pocket-sized one for free at any ticket office. https://content.tfl.gov.uk/standard-tube-map.pdf

Link to London Tube map

Best payment methods: Contactless payment is the winner for most tourists exploring London's Tube! Simply tap your credit card or phone on the yellow readers when entering <u>and</u> exiting, and enjoy automatic fare calculations with daily caps. <u>Important tip:</u> Everyone age 11 and older needs their own separate payment card or device for the Tube – no sharing allowed! The system can't distinguish between different passengers using the same card. Children under 11 travel free with a paying adult, so they don't need their own card.

Should you get an Oyster card? An Oyster card is only worth considering if you face hefty foreign transaction fees, need child discounts (ages 11-15), have multiple people traveling together or want the attraction discounts included with

Visitor Oyster cards. Both payment options charge identical fares with the same daily caps, so most travelers will find their contactless card the hassle-free choice — one less thing to juggle while exploring London's treasures! Just remember to always tap in and out with the same card.

Finding your platform is easier than you might think! Once you've tapped your card at the barriers (remember, you can use your contactless credit card or buy an Oyster card), follow the signs for your line. Specifically, look for signs showing the last station on your line in the direction you want to go - that's how platforms are labeled. For example, if you're taking the Central line east through London, you'd follow signs for "Central Line - Epping." If you're heading west, look for signs for "Central Line - West Ruislip." Still not sure? Don't worry - every station has friendly staff who are used to helping visitors find their way!

Now, about getting off at the right stop - there's a trick to this! Each carriage has a Tube map inside, and there are regular announcements telling you which station is next. <u>Pro tip:</u> most trains also have electronic displays showing the next station, and many now announce which side the doors will open on. If you're worried about missing your stop, try to sit near one of these displays, and start moving toward the doors a little before your station. And download the TfL (Transport for London) app - it's a lifesaver for planning routes and checking for any service disruptions!

When it comes to Tube etiquette, there are a few unwritten rules that'll help you blend in with the locals. The big one: stand on the right on escalators so people can walk past on the left (you'll definitely get some polite "excuse me's" if you forget this one!). During rush hour, take off your backpack and hold it by your feet to make more room. Let people off the train before you try to get on, and move down inside the carriages rather than clustering by the doors. If you're offered a seat by someone, it's perfectly fine to accept with a smile and a "thank you." And while Londoners might seem quiet on the Tube - reading or looking at their phones - they're usually happy to help if you need directions!

As for station amenities, you'll be pleasantly surprised! Most major stations have everything you might need for your journey - from coffee shops and small convenience stores to ATMs and restrooms (though heads up - they're called "toilets" here, and you might need to pay a small fee to use them). Many larger stations like King's Cross St. Pancras or Victoria have shopping areas with plenty of grab-and-go food options. You'll find ticket machines and staffed windows for buying tickets or getting help with your Oyster card, and there's usually a handy information board showing the status of all Tube lines. Most stations also have free WiFi - just look for the "Virgin Media WiFi" network and register once to get connected across the whole network. And if you're traveling late, don't worry - while the Tube isn't 24/7 like New York's subway, there are plenty of Night Tube services on weekends for many major lines!

Regional Differences in Transportation

Transportation in the UK isn't one-size-fits-all. In cities like London and Manchester, public transport is super robust, with buses, trams, and trains crisscrossing every neighborhood. But head to a rural area, and things slow down a bit (Cowie, 2017). Don't be surprised if buses run only a few times a day, or trains stop in tiny stations that are miles apart and that look straight out of a period drama.

Scotland, Wales, and Northern Ireland also have their own systems and quirks. For instance, Scotland's trains often pass through jaw-dropping landscapes, while Wales has some routes that take you right along the coast. Northern Ireland is smaller, so its train and bus network is more limited but still efficient. However, in these regions, renting a car might still be your best bet if you have your heart set on exploring off the beaten path.

Taxis and Ride-Sharing Services

Whether you're exploring charming local neighborhoods or venturing to scenic spots beyond the train lines, you'll want to know your options for getting around by taxi and car service in the UK.

Meet the Famous Black Cab

Let's talk about those iconic black taxis you've probably seen in movies. These aren't just any regular cabs - they're pretty special! The drivers are absolute wizards when it comes to knowing their way around (especially in London, where they have to pass an incredibly tough test called "The Knowledge"). Think of them as your local expert on wheels - they know all the shortcuts and can get you there faster by using special bus lanes. Feel free to ask them for recommendations for pubs or entertainment options.

Want to grab one? Just stick out your hand on the street or head to a taxi rank (that's British for "taxi stand") - you'll often find them outside train stations or major tourist spots. And here's a cool thing: every black cab can fit a wheelchair, which is super helpful if you need accessibility.

The More Budget-Friendly Option: Minicabs

If you're watching your pounds and pence, minicabs might be your new best friend. Think of them like a pre-booked car service back home. You can't flag them down on the street (that's a big no-no in the UK), but they're usually cheaper than black cabs. Just make sure to book them through a licensed company or app - it's the safe way to go!

Apps Make Life Easier

Just like back home, ride-sharing apps are super popular in UK cities. While you'll recognize Uber, you might want to check out some local favorites:

- Free Now: The locals love this one - you can get both regular taxis and private cars
- Bolt: Often a bit easier on the wallet than Uber
- Plus other car-hire services like Addison Lee if you're feeling fancy

Heading to the Countryside?

Here's where things get a bit trickier. If you're planning to explore those gorgeous rural areas (and you should!), keep in mind that taxis work differently out there:

- You'll want to book ahead - way ahead sometimes
- Ride-sharing apps might not be available
- Local taxi companies are your friends - research at home and save their numbers

Quick Tips for a Smooth Ride

- Keep some cash handy - not every cab takes cards.

- Save taxi company numbers in your phone.

- If you like a particular driver, ask if you can book future rides with them direct.

- Friday and Saturday nights get super busy - book ahead if you can, especially for a theatre or concert event.

Getting around by taxi in the UK is pretty straightforward once you know the basics. The drivers are generally friendly and helpful, and don't be shy about asking questions - most are happy to chat and might even share some local tips about where to get the best fish and chips!

Private Car Hire

Many travelers overlook one of the most convenient transport options in the UK—private car services that can take you literally anywhere across the country! While not the budget choice, hiring a private car delivers unmatched convenience for specific situations, like arriving late at night with mountains of luggage, traveling with elderly family members, or reaching that picture-perfect but supremely isolated countryside hotel – the peace of mind is simply priceless..

Companies like Addison Lee, Blacklane, and Uber Executive don't just handle London airport transfers—they'll happily drive you on those three-hour-plus journeys to remote destinations poorly served by public transport. Imagine being whisked away to a secluded Cotswolds cottage or Scottish Highlands retreat without navigating confusing train connections or unfamiliar roads!

Starting from £40 for short London trips and ranging into the hundreds for those cross-country adventures, private hire offers door-to-door service with the peace of mind that comes from having a pre-booked, guaranteed ride. Just remember to book well in advance, especially for those longer journeys where drivers often double as informal local guides to enhance your experience.

Renting Bicycles and Scooters

Feeling eco-friendly? Many cities offer bike and scooter rentals. In London, apps like Santander Cycles (aka "Boris Bikes") are available at docking stations throughout the city. Apps like Lime and Tier offer electric scooters in cities like Birmingham and Bristol. They're a fun and affordable way to explore the city, especially if you're sticking to parks or quieter streets.

Just remember to stay in designated cycling lanes, always wear a helmet, and follow traffic rules (Cowie, 2017).

Walking and Cycling in Cities

The UK is incredibly pedestrian- and cyclist-friendly. Cities like Oxford and Cambridge are famous for their bike culture, while places like Bath and York are a walker's paradise with their cobblestone streets and historic landmarks. Wear comfy shoes, and don't be afraid to get a little lost—it's part of the fun!

REALLY IMPORTANT SAFETY TIP: Traffic in the UK comes from the right, not the left, as Americans are used to. Train yourself by repeating "Look right, look left, look right" every time you cross a street. This small habit can help you stay safe and avoid accidents while exploring.

That about covers the short -distance travel, but what about those longer journeys? In the next chapter, we'll cover all about the UK train systems and how to plan a journey to just about anywhere!

Chapter Three

All Aboard! UK Train Travel

Hopping on a British train might just be the best decision you'll make on your UK adventure! Britain's extensive rail network connects practically every corner of this beautiful island, making it an absolute dream for travelers. Picture this: instead of stressing about driving on the "wrong" side of the road or navigating roundabouts, you're comfortably settled in your seat, maybe with a cup of tea and a scone, watching the British countryside unfold like a living postcard through your window. We're talking ancient stone walls criss-crossing emerald hills, sheep dotting the landscapes like tiny cotton balls, and charming villages with church spires peeking through the morning mist.

The best part? While you're soaking in these views, you're also traveling in one of the safest and most efficient ways possible - British railways have an impressive safety record and run like clockwork (most of the time!). Whether you're planning to zip from London to Edinburgh in just over four hours, explore the rugged coastline of Cornwall, or venture into the Scottish Highlands, the train offers something that no other mode of transport can match: the perfect blend of convenience, comfort, and pure travel magic. Plus, you'll be following in the footsteps of countless travelers who've been making these same journeys since the Victorian era - though thankfully, today's trains are a bit more comfortable than their 19th-century counterparts! Trust me, there's nothing quite like settling into your seat, pulling out your camera (or your book), and letting Britain's railways show you the very best of this incredible country.

Planning Your British Rail Adventure: Routes, Tickets, and Timetables

Let's dive into how to plan those train journeys like a pro! Trust me, while British train travel might seem complex at first glance, with these tips you will be able to navigate the system with confidence and plan the perfect itinerary.

Your Digital Travel Toolkit

Let's talk about the essential websites and apps that'll become your best friends while planning. The National Rail website (nationalrail.co.uk) is your go-to starting point - think of it as the Google of British train travel! This fantastic resource lets you check routes, times, and prices for any journey in Great Britain. You can download their app too. It's brilliant for real-time updates and platform information when you're actually traveling.

Want to get a bit more tech-savvy with your planning? The Trainline app (thetrainline.com) offers a super user-friendly interface that many visitors love. While they do charge a small booking fee, their journey planner is incredibly intuitive, especially if you're trying to piece together multiple trips. They'll even show you clever split-ticket options that could save you money (more on that money-saving trick later!).

Finding Your Perfect Route

Let's say you're dreaming of that classic journey from London to Edinburgh, or maybe you're intrigued by the idea of exploring Cornwall's picturesque coastline. Each train operator has their own website where you can dive deep into specific routes. For instance, LNER (London North Eastern Railway) handles those scenic east coast routes up to Scotland, while GWR (Great Western Railway) is your ticket to Cornwall and the West Country.

Here's a fun planning tip: use Google Maps in transit mode to get a visual sense of your route. It's a great way to spot interesting stops along the way or figure out possible day trips. For example, you might notice that Durham Cathedral is right on your way to Edinburgh - perfect for breaking up that journey with some medieval history!

Timing is Everything

Most train companies release their cheapest tickets around 12 weeks in advance, and you can set up alerts on their websites to notify you when these become available. But here's something many visitors don't realize: you can actually look up train times for any date, even before tickets go on sale. This is super helpful for planning your itinerary, especially if you're trying to coordinate multiple destinations.

Research Beyond the Railways

Don't forget to check out some brilliant third-party resources that can add extra depth to your planning:

- Seat61.com is fantastic for detailed route information and insider tips

- BritRail's website can help you decide if a rail pass might save you money

- Individual train company websites often have dedicated sections about scenic routes and tourist attractions along their lines

- Tripadvisor.com has UK specific forums with a wealth of information from other experienced travelers

- UKTravelPlanning.com is a fantastic resource for insider tips on train journeys and even have an extensive e-book with more extensive train travel tips

The Local Knowledge Advantage

Local tourist boards often have dedicated sections about traveling to their regions by train. Want to explore the Lake District? The Cumbria Tourism website has brilliant guides about reaching those gorgeous lakes and fells by rail. Planning a Highland adventure? Visit Scotland's website features some absolutely stunning rail journeys that'll have you dreaming of kilts and highland cows (or as the locals say, coos).

Remember, planning your rail journey isn't just about getting from A to B - it's about crafting an experience that'll become one of your favorite travel memories. Take time to research those scenic routes, check out station facilities (especially at connection points), and maybe even plan some stops at those charming towns you'll be passing through.

Mastering UK Train Tickets: Your Guide to Saving Money and Booking Smart

The British rail system, with its intricate network of routes and diverse ticket options, offers travelers a gateway to exploring the United Kingdom's historic cities and picturesque countryside. Understanding the nuances of ticket booking not only saves money but transforms what might seem a daunting process into a straightforward part of your British travel experience. Whether you're planning day trips to coastal towns or traversing the length of Great Britain, mastering these essential booking strategies will help you travel with the confidence and efficiency of a seasoned railway passenger.

The Art of Advance Booking

Train Station Boards

Here's one of the biggest secrets to UK train travel: timing is everything! British train fares work like airline tickets – prices change based on timing and demand. Book early (ideally 12 weeks before travel), and you could pay a fraction of the walk-up fare. For example, that London to Edinburgh journey I mentioned? Book it the day before, and you might spend £150 or more. But plan ahead, and you could snag it for as little as £30! The sweet spot for booking is usually between 8-12 weeks before travel, when those coveted "Advance" tickets first go on sale.

Understanding Ticket Types

Here's a breakdown of those sometimes confusing ticket options:

Advance Tickets:

- The cheapest option - but you're locked into a specific train
- Must be booked ahead (up to 12 weeks before travel)
- Perfect if your plans are set in stone
- Non-refundable, but can sometimes be changed for a fee

Off-Peak Tickets:

- More flexible - travel any time outside rush hours
- Usually valid after 9:30 AM on weekdays
- Great for day trips and leisure travel
- Can be bought on the day, but cheaper in advance

Anytime Tickets:

- The most expensive but most flexible option
- Use any train, any time
- Perfect if you need maximum flexibility
- Usually only worth it if your plans might change last-minute

The Magic of Railcards

Now, here's where it gets really interesting! Railcards are your secret weapon for saving money on British trains. Even as a visitor, you have several options that could save you a third off most fares:

For Solo Travelers:

- 16-25 Railcard (also available to full-time students of any age!)
- Senior Railcard (for those 60+)
- Network Railcard (perfect for exploring Southeast England)

For Group Travel:

- Two Together Railcard (ideal for couples - saves 33% when you travel together)
- Family & Friends Railcard (up to 4 adults and 4 kids can travel on one card)
- GroupSave (automatic discounts for groups of 3-9 adults traveling together)

Most railcards cost £30 for one year, but if you're planning several journeys, they often pay for themselves in just one or two trips! Even better? You can usually use them on London's Underground and local trains too.

Smart Booking Strategies

Here are some insider tips on getting the best deals:

Split Ticketing:

Sometimes, buying separate tickets for different parts of your journey works out cheaper than one through ticket. Websites like Trainline or Split My Fare can do this calculation for you automatically. Don't worry - you don't usually need to change trains, it's just a paper exercise!

Season Tickets:

Planning to explore one region intensively? Look into seasonal tickets or regional rovers.

The BritRail Pass unlocks Britain's entire rail network, letting you hop between bustling cities and charming villages with complete freedom. Available in durations from 3 days to a month, it's perfect for spontaneous adventurers who want to explore Britain's diverse landscapes - from Cornwall's rugged coastline to Scotland's misty highlands - all on a single ticket. These passes are exclusively for overseas visitors and can be fantastic value if you're planning multiple journeys. You'll need to buy them before you arrive in the UK, but they offer unlimited travel and the freedom to hop on and off trains as you please. Visit BritRail.com for all the info.

The Spirit of Scotland Travelpass is your golden ticket to unlimited rail adventures across Scotland's most spectacular landscapes, from the bustling streets of Edinburgh to the rugged shores of the Highlands. Available in flexible four or eight-day options, this pass lets you hop on and off ScotRail services at will, including some of the country's most scenic routes like the West Highland Line and the Kyle of Lochalsh railway. For travelers looking to immerse themselves in Scotland's raw beauty without the hassle of individual ticket booking, it's an absolute game-changer. Visit ScotRail.co.uk for more info.

Booking Your Tickets

You've got several options for actually buying your tickets:

Online Booking:

- Direct through train company websites (no booking fee)
- Through Trainline (small booking fee but great user interface)
- National Rail website (redirects to train companies)

At the Station:

- Ticket offices (staffed by helpful humans!)
- Self-service machines
- Some smaller stations might only have machines

Collecting Your Tickets:

Most tickets can be:
- Downloaded as e-tickets to your phone
- Collected from station machines using your booking reference
- Posted to your hotel or accommodation
- Some routes now accept contactless payment directly at the gate

Train Tickets

Station Information

British train stations come in all shapes and sizes, from the magnificent Victorian architecture of London's St Pancras to tiny rural platforms in Cornwall. Let's talk about what to expect at both ends of the spectrum.

Major City Stations

The big urban stations are practically shopping malls with trains! You'll find:

- Multiple food options, from grab-and-go to sit-down restaurants
- Shops selling everything from books to clothing
- Left luggage facilities for storing bags
- Ticket offices with actual humans to help you
- Clean toilets
- Free WiFi
- Waiting rooms
- ATMs
- Information boards showing departures and platforms

Rural Stations

Now, here's where it gets interesting! Smaller stations might have:

- A basic shelter or waiting room
- A ticket machine (but not always!)
- Basic information boards
- Maybe a small cafe or shop (emphasis on maybe)
- Possibly no staff at all
- Limited or no toilet facilities

Important note: if you're heading to a rural station, check if you need to buy tickets in advance. Some smaller stations don't have ticket facilities at all!

Really important note: Don't assume there will be a taxi service available. Be sure to book in advance for any transport from a train station outside of a major city.

Finding Your Train

Okay, you've got your ticket, you're at the station and you are ready to go! British stations use a platform system, and your train's platform usually isn't announced until about 10-15 minutes before departure. This can feel stressful at first, but don't worry - it's all part of the experience!

Keep an eye on the big departure boards. They'll show:

- Your train's scheduled time
- The final destination
- Major stops along the way

- The platform number (when announced)
- Any delays or disruptions

When your platform appears, follow the signs. In bigger stations, this might mean a bit of a walk and maybe some stairs or escalators. Don't panic if it seems like a long way - stations are well-sign posted, and there's usually plenty of time.

Understanding Your Ticket and Finding Your Seat

British train tickets can look a bit cryptic at first. They'll show:

- Your journey details
- Any restrictions on when you can travel
- Whether you have a seat reservation
- The class of travel (Standard or First)

About seat reservations: these are usually free when you book but aren't always mandatory. If you are picky about sitting facing forward or by a window, make sure to reserve a seat.

Some trains have unreserved cars where you can sit anywhere. How do you know which is which? Look for:

- Digital displays above seats showing reservations
- Paper tickets stuck to seat headrests
- Cars marked as "unreserved seating"
- Ask a train conductor which cars have available seating

If you don't have a reservation, look for the unreserved cars - they're usually marked with signs on the platform or on the train itself.

Train Etiquette: The Unwritten Rules

Every country has its train etiquette, and Britain is no exception. Here's how to travel like a local:

Quiet Cars:

- Some cars are designated as "Quiet Zones"
- No phone calls allowed

- Keep conversations hushed
- Headphones should be barely audible to others

General Etiquette:

- Keep your feet off the seats (seriously, this one's important!)
- Don't take up extra seats with your bags if the train's busy
- If someone has reserved the seat you're in, move without fuss
- It's perfectly fine to eat on trains, but nothing too smelly
- Clean up after yourself

The Great British Queue:

- British people love an orderly queue
- On busy platforms, people often line up where the doors will be
- Let people off before trying to board
- If you're not sure where to queue, just follow the locals!

Smart Luggage Storage:

- Most trains have overhead racks perfect for medium-sized suitcases and backpacks - they're free and right above your seat
- Look for the dedicated luggage areas at the ends of carriages for larger bags - just keep an eye on them during stops
- Short on space? Many major stations have left luggage facilities where you can store bags for a few hours or the whole day
- For day trips, consider station lockers - they're usually cheaper than staffed facilities and available 24/7
- If you're staying at a hotel, they'll often hold your bags even before check-in or after check-out - just ask nicely!

Special Journeys

Here are some iconic routes for an unforgettable train experience:

London to Scotland:

The major operators are LNER and Avanti West Coast, offering two distinct routes to Scotland that each have their own charm. The journey from London's Kings Cross Station to Edinburgh's Waverley Station takes about 4.5 hours along LNER's east coast route, and the views along the North Sea coastline are absolutely spectacular - keep your camera ready as you pass Durham Cathedral and cross the Royal Border Bridge! If Glasgow's your destination, Avanti West Coast will whisk you there in about 4.5 hours via the west coast route, treating you to gorgeous views of the Lake District and rolling hills of the Scottish Borders. Both routes offer excellent onboard services, including dining cars where you can enjoy a meal while watching Britain roll by your window - there's nothing quite like having afternoon tea as you speed through the countryside!

Cornwall:

GWR runs trains from London Paddington to Cornwall, following one of Britain's most celebrated railway routes. It's a beautiful journey, but be prepared - it's about 5 hours to Penzance, winding through some of England's most picturesque countryside. The views of the Devon coast make it worthwhile, especially the stunning stretch along the sea wall at Dawlish where the tracks run right alongside the ocean! Don't forget to grab a seat on the left side of the train heading down for the best coastal views, and keep an eye out for the magnificent Brunel Bridge as you cross into Cornwall - it's an engineering marvel that'll take your breath away.

Northern Ireland:

Here's something important to know: Northern Ireland has a separate rail system, operating independently from the rest of the UK. You'll need to either fly or take a ferry - many visitors enjoy the ferry crossing from Liverpool or Scotland as a mini-adventure in itself! If you're planning to explore by rail once you're there, book through Translink, Northern Ireland's transport operator, which offers scenic routes like the stunning coastal journey from Belfast to Derry/Londonderry. The trains in Northern Ireland might be fewer than on the mainland, but they're modern, comfortable, and connect all the major tourist destinations - plus the views of the Antrim coast are simply unforgettable.

Wales:

Transport for Wales operates most Welsh routes, offering everything from quick city hops to epic scenic journeys through the mountains. The Cardiff to Swansea route is popular with tourists, serving as a perfect gateway to explore South Wales's beautiful coastline, and the Heart of Wales line offers some breathtaking scenery as it winds through remote valleys and historic market towns. For a truly memorable experience, take the Cambrian Coast Line from Machynlleth to Pwllheli - it hugs the coastline with mountains on one side and the Irish Sea on the other, offering what many consider to be some of the most spectacular railway views in all of Britain!

On-Board Experience

What can you expect during your journey? Most long-distance trains offer:

- Toilets (usually at least one per car)
- Power outlets for charging devices
- Tables or fold-down trays
- Food and drink service (either trolley service or a cafe car)
- WiFi (quality varies!)

First Class vs. Standard Class:

Is First Class worth it? It depends. You'll get:

- Wider seats
- More legroom
- Complimentary food and drinks on some services
- Quieter carriages
- Power outlets at every seat

The price difference can be substantial, but watch for weekend upgrades - some operators offer cheap First Class upgrades on Saturdays and Sundays.

Dealing with Disruptions

British trains generally run well, but delays happen. Good to know:

- Most stations announce disruptions clearly
- Major stations have help desks for assistance

- Train company apps usually show live updates
- If you're delayed by more than 15-30 minutes (depending on the operator), you might be entitled to compensation
- Staff are usually very helpful if you're not sure what to do

Taking the Eurostar to Paris

Want to hop over to Paris for a few days? The most exciting ways to travel between two of Europe's greatest cities is the Eurostar! This sleek high-speed train service whisks you from the heart of London (St Pancras International) to the center of Paris (Gare du Nord) in just 2 hours and 15 minutes - faster than flying when you consider all that airport hassle! You'll want to arrive at St Pancras at least 45 minutes before departure for security and passport control (remember, you're crossing an international border!), but the process is usually much smoother than at airports. Important fact – Paris time is one hour later than London time, so adjust your itineraries accordingly!

Now, let's talk about the most incredible part of your journey - traveling through the Channel Tunnel, or "Chunnel" as it's affectionately known! About 20 minutes into your trip, you'll begin the fascinating 20-minute journey through this engineering marvel that runs deep beneath the English Channel. Don't worry if you're a bit nervous about underwater travel - the tunnel is incredibly safe and so smooth you might not even realize you're 250 feet below the seabed! While you won't see fish swimming by (you're in a solid tunnel, after all!), it's quite an experience to think about the fact that you're traveling through the world's longest underwater tunnel while sipping your coffee or reading a book.

Book your tickets as early as possible on the Eurostar website - prices start around £39 each way if you snag those early deals, but can climb to £200+ if you wait until the last minute. You can take two suitcases and a piece of hand luggage with no extra fees, and there are no liquid restrictions like on flights. Pro tip: treat yourself to Standard Premier class if you can - you'll get a light meal served at your seat and more legroom, perfect for watching the French countryside zip by at 186 mph once you emerge from the tunnel. Keep your camera ready - the transition from English to French landscapes is fascinating, and before you know it, you'll be pulling into the bustling Gare du Nord, ready to start your Parisian adventure!

All Aboard for Magic: Britain's Most Spectacular Steam Train Journeys

No chapter about train travel in Britain is complete without mentioning some of the most enchanting rail experiences - the kind that'll transport you not just across the countryside, but back in time! While modern trains are great for getting from A to B, there's something absolutely magical about climbing aboard a historic steam train and watching the countryside unfold at a more leisurely pace. These journeys aren't just trips, they're time machines wrapped in steam and nostalgia!

The Hogwarts Express Come to Life: The Jacobite Steam Train

Jacobite Steam Train

Let's start with the crown jewel of British steam journeys - the famous Jacobite Steam Train in Scotland. You might recognize this gorgeous route as the Hogwarts Express from the Harry Potter films, and the real thing is just as magical! Running from Fort William to Mallaig, this 84-mile round trip takes you through some of Scotland's most spectacular scenery. The highlight? Crossing the magnificent Glenfinnan Viaduct, with its towering arches curving through the highlands. Book well ahead - this journey sells out months in advance, especially in summer. Pro tip: snag a seat on the left side heading out for the best views of the viaduct, and don't miss afternoon tea in the dining car!

Yorkshire's Timeless Wonder: North Yorkshire Moors Railway

Fancy stepping into the heart of James Herriot country? The North Yorkshire Moors Railway offers one of Britain's most charming day trips. Winding through the stunning North York Moors National Park from Pickering to Whitby, you'll chug past heather-covered hills, ancient villages, and filming locations from the Harry Potter films and All Creatures Great and Small. Make time to explore Whitby when you arrive - this historic seaside town, with its abbey ruins and connection to Dracula, is worth the journey alone!

Welsh Highland Railway: Mountains and Maritime Magic

For a truly spectacular narrow-gauge experience, hop aboard the Welsh Highland Railway in Eryri National Park (also called Snowdonia). Starting in the shadow of Caernarfon Castle, this remarkable journey takes you through the heart of Wales's highest mountains, past the foot of Yr Wyddfa (also called Snowdon) itself, and through the stunning Aberglaslyn Pass. The carriages are beautifully restored, and some even offer first-class observation cars with panoramic windows. Pack a picnic to enjoy at one of the scenic stops along the way!

The Dartmouth Steam Railway: The English Riviera Express

Want to combine a steam journey with a boat trip? The Dartmouth Steam Railway in Devon offers just that! This beautiful route along the English Riviera coast includes some of the most stunning coastal views you'll find anywhere in Britain. The Round Robin ticket combines your steam train journey with a river cruise and vintage bus ride - it's three classic forms of transport in one perfect day out! As you chug along in your vintage carriage, you'll pass through charming seaside towns, spot boats bobbing in picturesque harbors, and maybe even catch dolphins playing in the waves if you're lucky.

Planning Your Steam Adventure

A few insider tips for making the most of these historic journeys:

- Book well in advance, especially for the Jacobite
- Many railways offer dining experiences - they're worth the splurge!
- Check seasonal timetables - some services run more frequently in summer

- Pack layers - these historic carriages can be chilly, even in summer
- Bring your camera - the photo opportunities are endless
- Consider a first-class ticket for the best views and most comfortable seats

Each of these journeys offers something unique, whether it's breathtaking scenery, historic charm, or just the pure joy of traveling behind a steam locomotive. They're more than just train rides - they're windows into Britain's golden age of rail travel, and trust me, there's nothing quite like the sound of a steam whistle echoing across the hills or the sight of steam billowing past your window as you curve through the countryside.

British train travel can seem complicated at first, but it's actually a fantastic way to see the country. You'll get to enjoy the changing landscapes, chat with locals, and experience Britain's proud railway heritage firsthand. Plus, there's something magical about pulling into a station that's been welcoming travelers for over 150 years. So grab your ticket, find your platform, and get ready for an adventure on Britain's railways!

Chapter Four

Driving in the UK

So, you've tackled the buses and conquered the trains, and now you're ready for the ultimate travel freedom—driving! If you're dreaming of rolling countryside, historic villages, and beautiful coastal routes, renting a car is the perfect way to experience the UK's hidden gems.

But driving here is a little different from what you're used to in the US. Don't worry, though—we've got you fully covered! In this chapter, we'll walk you through the essentials, from understanding UK driving laws to discovering scenic routes, so you can drive with total confidence. Before you know it, you'll be zipping through charming country lanes, navigating roundabouts like a local, and even mastering the art of parallel parking on those characteristically narrow British streets!

Ready to hit the road? Let's get started!

Understanding UK Driving Laws and Regulations

Before you grab the keys, it's important to know the rules of the road. While the UK's driving laws might feel familiar to American drivers, there are some key differences to keep in mind:

Driving License Requirements

Your US driver's license is valid in the UK for up to 12 months (Svaiko, 2023). However, some rental companies may require an International Driving Permit (IDP), especially if you plan to visit Scotland's remote areas or Northern Ireland. You can get an IDP at AAA offices, which is currently the only authorized outlet for IDPs in the US.

Seat Belts and Child Safety

- It's a legal requirement for everyone in the car to wear a seat belt, whether in the front or back (Svaiko, 2023).
- If children are traveling with you, they must use a child car seat unless they are over 12 years old or taller than 135 cm (about 4'5").

Phone Use While Driving

Using your phone while driving is strictly prohibited unless it's hands-free. Even holding your phone at a red light can result in fines!

Drunk-Driving Laws

The legal blood alcohol limit in England, Wales, and Northern Ireland is 80 mg per 100 ml of blood, but in Scotland, it's stricter at 50 mg per 100 ml of blood (*The Drink Drive Limit*). For most visitors, the safest rule is simple: *Don't drink and drive*.

> For more detailed guidance on UK driving laws, you can visit the official Highway Code website at https://www.highwaycodeuk.co.uk/.

Differences Between US and UK Driving

One of the first things you'll notice when driving in the UK is that it's not just the steering wheel that's on the "wrong" side—it's the entire road! Driving on the left-hand side of the road is one of the most significant adjustments for American drivers (Svaiko, 2023). Vehicles in the UK have the steering wheel on the right-hand side, which might feel awkward initially but will soon become second nature.

Another major difference lies in the design of the roads. While American roads tend to be wider and more spacious, many UK roads—particularly in rural areas and historic towns—are much narrower (Reynolds, 2021). Single-track roads with passing areas called "lay-bys" are common in the countryside, and it's important to be patient and give way to oncoming traffic when necessary. And don't forget to smile and give a little wave to the other driver when you pass by.

The traffic management system also differs, with roundabouts replacing many four-way stops and traffic signals. While roundabouts might seem daunting at first, they are designed to keep traffic flowing smoothly and are easy to navigate with a little practice (more on this later).

Lastly, parking spaces in the UK are often smaller than their US counterparts, reflecting the smaller size of most vehicles. When renting a car, if your passengers and luggage needs allow it, consider opting for a compact model to make parking easier, especially in cities.

Driving on the Left: Tips and Adjustments

Adjusting to driving on the left side of the road can be challenging, particularly if it's your first time. The most important thing to remember is to stay calm and focus. With these few adjustments, you'll quickly adapt to this new way of driving.

Start Small

A great way to ease into driving on the left is to start your journey in a less congested area. Avoid jumping straight into city traffic and instead practice in a quiet town or rural setting where you can focus on the basics without feeling rushed.

Keep Left Reminders

Keeping a reminder to "Keep left" on your dashboard can also be helpful, especially when making turns or merging onto a new road. Remember that oncoming traffic will be on your right, which might feel counterintuitive at first.

Passenger Assistance

One of the trickiest aspects of driving on the left is navigating roundabouts and intersections. Take your time when approaching these, and always double-check that you're entering on the correct side of the road. If you're traveling with someone, enlist them as your co-pilot. They can help with navigation, spotting signs, and reminding you to stay on the left.

Navigating Roundabouts and Other Unique UK Road Features

Roundabouts might seem tricky at first, but they're simpler than they look and help to keep traffic moving. Here's how to conquer them like a pro:

1. **Yield to the right:** Traffic already in the roundabout has the right of way, so, as you approach, slow down, check to your right, and enter when it's safe.

2. **Signal correctly:** Inside the roundabout, signal clearly when you're ready to exit, avoiding confusion. Use your left turn signal when exiting the roundabout. If you're taking the first exit, stay in the left lane and signal left early. For other exits, follow the signs and lane markings.

3. **Don't stop:** Once in the roundabout, keep moving until you get to your exit.

4. **Don't panic:** Take your time and go around again if you miss your exit—there's no penalty for circling back!

Other features to look watch for:

- Be on the lookout for zebra pedestrian crossings, marked by black and white stripes. Pedestrians always have the right of way here, so be ready to stop if someone's waiting to cross.

- In rural areas, you might suddenly find yourself on a narrow or even single-lane roads, with visions of being stuck head-to-head with an oncoming car. But keep an eye out for passing areas called lay-bys. These spots, often marked by signs, allow vehicles to pass each other safely. Be considerate and use these places to let others go by when needed. Sometimes you might have to back up a bit to get to the nearest lay-by. Again, just stay calm, go slowly, and be courteous, and it will all work out.

- The UK enforces speed limits with speed cameras, so it would be wise to stick to the speed limit to avoid fines (more info later).

- Speed bumps are also common in residential areas. Always slow down when approaching them.

Renting a Car: Requirements, Tips, and Insurance

Renting a car in the UK isn't much different than in the US. Companies like *Enterprise*, *Avis*, *Arnold Clark*, and *Hertz* have locations across the country, including airports (Department for Transport, 2024). Here's some tips to get you started:

Things to know before renting:

- You'll need a valid US driver's license.

- An International Driving Permit (IDP) is recommended (and sometimes required if you're planning to visit rural Scotland or Northern Ireland—check with your rental company). Obtain this at a local AAA office before your trip.

- Check with your auto insurance company about coverage for your international rental. A few credit cards include insurance on international car rental – check out your options well before you leave for your trip to make sure you have full auto insurance coverage. This might be a time when you buy that extra insurance with the rental company, just to be safe.

- Really important tip: Automatic transmission cars are far less common than manual (stick-shift) ones in the U.K. Even if you know how to drive a manual, it's highly recommended to reserve an automatic car when booking. With all the other changes going on in the car, you don't need to worry about shifting gears. So, give yourself one less thing to worry about and make your driving experience much smoother by sticking with an automatic vehicle!

Prepping Like a Pro

Before you hit the gas, start with a little homework and prepare in advance. There are many YouTube videos that try to give you the experience of driving in the UK, and this is a great place to start. There are also websites like **Tripiamo.com** that offer extensive courses on UK driving, including tutorials on road signs and street markings, traffic laws, navigating roundabouts, as well as hours of video of real-life UK driving (Collins, 2025). These can be well worth the small fee to give you the knowledge and confidence to comfortably drive in Britain.

Ways to Plan Your Rental

According to the research (*How to Rent a Car: What to Know Before Renting a Car*), when it comes to renting a car (or car hire as it is called in Britain), you've got options. You can pick up your car right at the airport, you can take public transport to another hub and pick up your car there, or you travel to multiple hubs by public transport, and rent a different car in each city. Each comes with its perks and quirks, so pick the one that suits your itinerary.

Pick Up at the Airport

The first option is to pick up your car right at the airport and drive for your entire vacation. This may seem the most convenient option, but there are several problems with this plan:

- It is extremely inadvisable to drive in London. *Repeat:* **Do not drive in London**. There is no need for it, and it is not worth the hassle and expense. There are zones within London that do not allow non-electric cars, and anyone driving in these zones can face hefty fines. Use public transportation or taxis when in London.

- Renting directly from the airport, especially at Heathrow, can be unwise because this is a very busy area, and it might be quite confusing to have to navigate these highways while first getting used to driving on the left.

- Most flights from the US are overnight flights, and you are probably a bit tired. It's better to tackle driving after at least one good night's sleep.

Take Public Transport First

Considering spending a few days in London first, and then taking a train to another area and renting a car from there. It is best to create an itinerary that will bring you back to your destination so you can return the car to the same place (otherwise additional fees will occur to return the car to a different location).

Picking the Perfect Ride

When choosing a rental company and a car, there are a few key things to keep in mind. The first is that you should be sure to reserve an automatic transmission. Sorry I sound like a track on repeat but it is very important. Even if you can smoothly shift from a 0 to 65 in 9.4 seconds before your morning coffee in the US, it is definitely different using the shift stick on your left hand. Always rent an automatic transmission car.

Secondly, be careful to choose the right size car for your needs. If you choose a vehicle that is too small, you will find that you don't have enough room for your passengers and luggage. But if you have a car that is too large, you may find it awkward to drive down narrow lanes and park in small parking spaces. Also, car models have different names in the UK than in the US (The Nissan Qashqai, for example, is similar to the American Nissan Rogue). Do a little research on the car options you are given before making your reservation.

There is third option to be aware of when reserving your vehicle – whether to choose a gas-powered vs an electric car. Sometimes the automatic electric cars are a little less expensive than the gas (petrol) option. Renting electric has it's pros and cons. While most towns will have charging stations, they may be difficult to find, be out of order, or have a line to charge. Charging can take upwards of 60 minutes or more, so might not be a great option if you are on a tight schedule. On the pro side, sometimes you can get a great parking spot for an electric car, and charge your car while having your lunch or overnight at your hotel. And with petrol about twice as expensive in the UK compared to the US, electric charging might be cheaper overall and more eco-friendly.

Understanding Road Signs and Rules

Your first stop should be to visit The Highway Code website on UK Government website: https://www.gov.uk/guidance/the-highway-code/traffic-signs. There you can download a very helpful PDF that reviews all the traffic signs and their meanings.

UK road signs are designed to be intuitive, but they may look unfamiliar to American drivers as they rely heavily on symbols rather than text. Here are some important ones:

- **Circular signs:** Red circles indicate restrictions, such as speed limits or no entry, while blue circles provide mandatory instructions like "Turn left."

- **Triangular signs:** These are used for warnings, such as sharp bends or animal crossings.

- **Rectangular signs:** These are used to provide information, such as parking information.

Speed Limits

Speed limits are measured in miles per hour (mph) in the UK, but the signage might not be as prominent as in the US. You may see these speed limit signs with the red circle with a number inside.

Speed Limit

But you may also only see this sign – a black circle with a diagonal line. This is the National Speed Limit sign, and the speed limit will depend on the type of road you are traveling on. According to *Speed Limits*, look out for these common limits:

National Speed Limit

- 30 mph in towns and cities (urban areas)

- 60 mph on single-lane roads (rural areas)

- 70 mph on motorways (highways) and dual carriageways

Be aware of widespread speed cameras that strictly enforce speed limits. Fines apply to all drivers, including tourists, so watch for signs and follow posted limits. Another handy reference can be found here: https://www.gov.uk/government/publications/know-your-traffic-signs/speed-limit-signs

Scenic Driving Routes

One of the joys of driving in the UK is the opportunity to explore its stunning scenic driving routes. Some of the most iconic drives include the North Coast 500 in Scotland, a loop that takes you through breathtaking Highland landscapes; the Causeway Coastal Route in Northern Ireland, with views of rugged cliffs and the Giant's Causeway; and the charming Cotswolds, where winding roads lead to idyllic villages with honey-colored stone cottages. Spend time planning your route at home using a variety of web sites dedicated to that purpose. And although Google and Apple Maps are available throughout Britain, you might want to consider bringing along some paper maps to help with the navigation or any last-minute detours.

Parking Tips

When it comes to parking, it's best to use designated car parks whenever possible. These are marked and often safer than street parking. Pay attention to signs indicating time limits and fees, and avoid parking on double yellow lines, which usually signify no parking at any time (*Searching for Parking Costs the UK £23.3 Billion a Year*, 2017).

Like in the US, you will find that you can pay for parking using a credit card or mobile app. You might have to download an app to pay for your parking, as not all places will accept cash or cards.

Emergency Procedures

Finally, it's important to know what to do in case of an emergency. The UK's emergency number is 999, and for non-urgent police matters, you can dial 101 (Department for Science, Innovation and Technology et al., 2021). If you experience a breakdown, many rental companies include roadside assistance, or you can contact organizations like the AA (Automobile Association) or RAC.

In the event of an accident, stop your vehicle immediately, exchange insurance details with the other driver, and notify your rental company as soon as possible. Taking photos of the scene can also be helpful for insurance purposes.

With these tips and a bit of preparation, driving in the UK will be a breeze. You'll enjoy the freedom to explore at your own pace and the satisfaction of mastering a new set of driving skills. So hop in, buckle up, and let the adventure begin!

Chapter Five

Money Matters

Traveling abroad always brings up the big question: "How will I manage my money?" If you're heading to the UK, no need to fret—we've got all the tips and tricks to help you navigate British pounds, handle payments, tipping, taxes, and saving money. Managing your finances can be a breeze; with a bit of prep, you'll be strutting around like a savvy local in no time!

Currency: Understanding Pounds and Pence

The currency in the United Kingdom is the British Pound Sterling (GBP), often just called the pound. The symbol for the pound is £, and it's divided into 100 smaller units called pence (p) (*British money and currency*). It works in much the same way as in the US. For example, £1.50 means one pound and fifty pence.

The coins in circulation include 1p, 2p, 5p, 10p, 20p, 50p, £1, and £2, while the notes (or bills) are £5, £10, £20, and £50. It's important to note that Scotland also issues its banknotes, which look different but are still valid throughout the UK. Some places in England, however, may not be familiar with Scottish notes, so it's worth sticking to Bank of England notes where possible.

Coins of Britain

Some tips to quickly tell the coins apart:

- The coins that are silver in middle with gold on the outside are £1 and £2 coins, with the larger one being the two-pound coin.

- The heptagon (7-sided) coins are 50 p (larger), and 20 p (smaller).

- The round silver coins are 10 p (larger) and 5 p (smaller).

- The copper-colored coins (like US pennies) are 2 p (larger) and 1 p (smaller).

An Illustration of the Current Money of the UK

British paper currency is quite colorful, with the £20, £10, and £5 notes used most frequently. Having a mix of both notes and coins will make navigating small purchases and transactions much easier. It's worth noting that newer banknotes now feature the image of King Charles III, marking a change from the longstanding tradition of displaying Queen Elizabeth II.

U.K. Paper Currency

Exchanging Money: Best Practices

When it comes to exchanging your money for pounds, not all methods are created equal. To get the best rates and avoid excessive fees, follow these tips:

- **Exchange before you travel:** It's always smart to exchange at least a small amount of money before you leave home. Many banks and credit unions in the US offer competitive exchange rates and low fees. Having pounds on hand for taxis, snacks, or emergencies upon arrival is always a good idea.

- **Avoid airport exchanges:** Currency exchange kiosks at airports are notoriously expensive. They charge high fees and offer unfavorable rates. Unless you're stuck, avoid these at all costs.

- **Use ATMs upon arrival:** Once you're in the UK, ATMs (cash points) are one of the easiest and most cost-effective ways to get pounds. Stick to ATMs operated by banks (rather than independent ones in convenience stores), as they typically have lower fees. Be sure to check with your home bank about any foreign transaction fees before you travel.

- Try to avoid carrying too much cash. Credit and debit cards are widely accepted across the UK, including contactless payment options like Apple Pay and Google Pay (*British Money and Currency*). Around £30-£50 cash should be enough for offering quick purchases or small tips (more on tipping below).

- **Credit and debit cards:** Using your credit card for most transactions can save you time and hassle, but make sure your card doesn't charge foreign transaction fees. Many travel-focused cards, like the Chase Sapphire Preferred or Capital One Venture, offer no-fee international usage.

- **Avoid dynamic currency conversion:** When paying by card, you may be asked whether you'd like to be charged in your home currency (e.g., dollars) or pounds. <u>Always choose pounds</u>. Being charged in your home currency, known as Dynamic Currency Conversion, comes with hidden fees and a poor exchange rate.

Banking and ATMs: Accessibility and Fees

Accessing cash in the UK is easy, thanks to the abundance of ATMs located in cities, towns, and even rural areas. Banks like Barclays, HSBC, and NatWest have ATMs in most high streets, shopping centers, and transportation hubs. The great news? Many ATMs in the UK don't charge withdrawal fees, especially those operated by major banks.

However, some independent ATMs, especially in convenience stores or small shops, may charge a withdrawal fee. This fee will be displayed before you proceed with the transaction, so you'll always have the choice to cancel (*British money and currency*).

If you're using a US debit or credit card, check with your bank in advance about foreign transaction fees or daily withdrawal limits. Some cards may also require you to notify them about your trip to avoid being flagged for suspicious activity. For seamless transactions, consider using a travel-friendly bank account, such as Charles Schwab, which reimburses international ATM fees.

Tipping Etiquette in Restaurants and Services

Tipping in the UK is a bit different from what you might be used to in the US. According to (Arfin, 2024), here's what you need to know :

- **Restaurants:** Tipping is appreciated, but not mandatory in most restaurants. A service charge of 10-12.5% is often automatically added to your bill, so always check before leaving extra. If a service charge is included, you don't need to tip unless you feel the service was exceptional. If there's no service charge, a tip of 10-15% is customary.

- **Bars and pubs:** Tipping isn't expected at bars or pubs. When ordering drinks, you simply pay the amount due. However, if you've had excellent service, it's a nice gesture to say, "Have one for yourself," which means you're offering to pay for a small drink for the bartender.

- **Taxis:** Round up the fare to the nearest pound, or add 10% for longer journeys. For example, if the fare is £17.60, you could give the driver £18 or £19.

- **Hotels:** It's polite to tip hotel porters £1-2 per bag and leave a small tip of £2-5 for housekeeping staff at the end of your stay.

- **Tour guides:** If you take a guided tour, it's common to tip your guide £5-10, especially for a full-day tour or exceptional service.

For other services like hairdressers, tipping is appreciated but not mandatory.

Understanding VAT and Tax Refunds for Tourists

The UK has a Value Added Tax (VAT) of 20% on most goods and services. The good news? As a tourist, you may be eligible for a tax refund on purchases over a certain amount (*Tax on Shopping and Services*). Here's how it works:

1. **Shop at participating stores:** Look for shops displaying a "Tax-Free Shopping" sign. When you make a purchase, ask the retailer for a VAT refund form. You'll need to show your passport as proof that you're a visitor.

2. **Complete the refund process:** Before leaving the UK, take your completed VAT refund forms and receipts to the airport's customs desk. They will stamp your forms, which you can then submit to the refund

company. Refunds can be issued to your card or as cash, though cash refunds may incur additional fees.

3. **Plan ahead:** Keep in mind that not all items are eligible for VAT refunds (e.g., food and books), and the process can take some time. Arrive at the airport early if you plan to claim a refund.

Budgeting Tips for Travelers

Traveling in the UK can be expensive, but smart budgeting can help stretch your pounds. Here are a few tips:

- **Use contactless payment:** Many shops, cafés, and even public transport (like buses and the London Underground) accept contactless payments. It's fast, convenient, and eliminates the need to carry large amounts of cash. Contactless payment includes tap credit cards or Apple or Google Pay from your phone.

- **Travel off-peak:** Train fares, attractions, and even accommodations are often cheaper during off-peak hours or seasons. Plan your trip accordingly.

- **Take advantage of free attractions:** Many UK museums, parks, and historical landmarks are free to enter, such as the British Museum in London or the National Museum of Scotland in Edinburgh.

- **Meal deals:** Supermarkets like Tesco and Sainsbury's offer affordable meal deals, including a sandwich, snack, and drink for just a few pounds—a great option for lunch on the go.

Money-Saving Passes

- If you're planning to check off multiple attractions, consider purchasing one of the following passes to save both time and money:

  - **The London Pass:** With access to over 80 attractions (like the Tower of London and Westminster Abbey), it's perfect for first-time visitors to the capital. https://londonpass.com/en

  - **Historic Houses Membership:** Love castles, manors, and stately homes? This pass grants entry to over 300 historic properties, many of which are privately owned and less crowded. https://www.historichouses.org/

- **National Trust Membership:** Perfect for exploring the UK's natural beauty and historical estates. Think rolling hills, seaside cliffs, and charming gardens. https://www.nationaltrust.org.uk/membership/joining-from-the-usa

- (Pro tip: These passes often include guidebooks or apps to help plan your day—and some let you skip the queues!)

With all these tips and insights, you're all set to handle pounds, pence, and payments like a pro. Whether it's exchanging money smartly, mastering tipping etiquette, or understanding VAT, managing your finances in the UK doesn't have to be a headache.

Happy budgeting, and remember: Every penny saved is another pound to spend on your next adventure!

Chapter Six

Communication and Connectivity

Let's face it—staying connected while traveling is essential. Whether it's keeping in touch with family and friends, navigating your way with maps, sharing your travel photos online, or even staying updated on local news, knowing how to access mobile networks, the internet, and postal services can make your trip so much easier (and more fun!). Luckily, the UK has excellent connectivity options. This chapter will guide you through everything you need to know about staying connected in the UK—without breaking the bank or losing your cool.

Mobile Networks and Getting a UK SIM Card

When visiting the United Kingdom from the United States, staying connected is both easier and more affordable than many travelers expect. The UK boasts an extensive, reliable mobile network system that provides excellent coverage throughout the country. For stays longer than a few days, purchasing a local SIM card can significantly reduce your communication costs compared to international roaming charges.

Before your trip, the most crucial step is ensuring your phone is unlocked by contacting your US mobile carrier. Most modern smartphones from major carriers can be unlocked once they're paid off, though some carriers may have additional requirements. You'll also want to confirm your phone supports GSM networks, which is the standard used in the UK. If you're unsure about your phone's status, contact your provider well before your departure date to avoid any last-minute complications.

The UK's mobile landscape is dominated by four major network providers: EE, Vodafone, O2, and Three. Each offers pay-as-you-go (PAYG) options that are ideal for travelers, eliminating the need for long-term contracts or commitments. These providers compete vigorously on price and features, often offering generous data allowances and EU roaming capabilities. Basic plans start around £10, while more comprehensive packages with larger data allowances typically range from £20-50.

You can purchase SIM cards from an impressive variety of locations throughout the UK. Airport shops, convenience stores, supermarkets, and dedicated mobile carrier shops all stock them. Major retailers like WHSmith, Boots, and Tesco also offer SIM cards, making it convenient to get connected as soon as you arrive. The SIM packages typically include clear instructions for activation, which usually involves either making a call or visiting the carrier's website.

SIM Card

For those with newer smartphones, eSIM technology offers an even more convenient option. eSIMs allow you to download a mobile plan directly to your device without handling physical SIM cards. Major UK providers like EE and Vodafone offer eSIM options, which you can set up before even leaving home. This modern alternative is particularly appealing for tech-savvy travelers who prefer a seamless setup process.

Installing a physical SIM card remains straightforward: locate your phone's SIM tray (usually on the side of your device), use the provided SIM ejector tool or a paperclip to pop it out, replace your US SIM with the UK one, and restart your phone. Most UK SIM cards are now "trio-SIMs" that can be adjusted to fit any size slot (standard, micro, or nano). After insertion, follow the activation instructions provided with your purchase.

IMPORTANT: *Store your US SIM card somewhere safe where you won't forget or lose it. You will need to replace it when you touchdown in the US.*

Remember that switching to a UK SIM means you'll have a new UK phone number. To maintain accessibility, consider forwarding your US number to a service like Google Voice before departure, or check if your US carrier offers international Wi-Fi calling features. Many travelers rely on messaging apps like WhatsApp or Signal that work over data, making it easy to stay in touch with people back home regardless of which SIM you're using.

If you happen to have an old phone tucked away in a drawer somewhere, here's a handy trick: pop a UK SIM card into it and use it as a portable Wi-Fi hotspot for your main phone. You can then connect your regular phone, tablet, or laptop to this hotspot just like you would with regular Wi-Fi. It's a clever way to keep all your devices connected while only paying for one data plan!

If you prefer to stick with your US carrier, investigate their international roaming options before traveling. Many US providers offer daily travel passes for a flat fee (typically around $10 per day) or pay-as-you-go international rates. However, be cautious with this approach – these charges can accumulate quickly, especially for longer stays, large families or heavy data usage. For trips lasting more than a few days, a local UK SIM card usually provides better value for money and more generous data allowances.

Internet Access, VPNs, and Wi-Fi Availability

Wi-Fi is practically everywhere in the UK, making it easy to stay online even if you don't have a SIM card. Cafés, restaurants, hotels, shopping malls, and libraries almost always offer free Wi-Fi. Popular chain spots like Starbucks, Pret A Manger, and Costa Coffee are great go-to options when you're out and about.

Many cities have public Wi-Fi hotspots that keep you connected as you explore. London, for example, has extensive networks like The Cloud and BT Wi-Fi, which pop up all over the city. You may need to register or log in with your email, but after that, you're good to go.

Even better, many hotels include Wi-Fi as part of their room rate, but in some budget accommodations, you may need to pay a small access fee. If internet connectivity is important to you, make sure to check the Wi-Fi details before booking.

Public Transport Wi-Fi

Some trains and buses even have free Wi-Fi. For example, most National Express coaches and trains like LNER offer free connectivity while you're traveling. Just remember that these networks can be a little slow during peak times, so don't expect to stream movies on your train ride.

Virtual Private Networks (VPNs)

While you'll find free Wi-Fi almost everywhere in the UK, it's worth being smart about how you use these public networks. They're fantastic for basic browsing and checking social media, but think twice before logging into sensitive accounts like your bank or email. Public Wi-Fi networks can be a bit like having a conversation in a crowded room - you never know who might be listening!

This is where a VPN (Virtual Private Network) comes in really handy. Think of a VPN as your own personal security tunnel through the internet. It encrypts all your data, making it unreadable to anyone trying to snoop on your online activity. Popular services like Surfshark, NordVPN, or ExpressVPN are easy to use - just download their app before your trip, hit connect when you're using public Wi-Fi, and you're good to go. Most VPNs cost around $10-15 per month, though you can often find better deals if you sign up for longer periods. Many also offer free trials, so you could set one up just for your UK trip.

A VPN has some other perks too - it can help you access your favorite streaming services from home (though this isn't guaranteed), and some UK websites might work better with a VPN if they get confused by your foreign location. Just remember to download and set up your VPN before leaving home, as it can be trickier to do once you're already abroad and trying to use unfamiliar networks. Better safe than sorry when it comes to keeping your personal information secure while traveling!

Portable Wi-Fi Devices

If you want to skip the whole SIM card shuffle and need reliable internet for multiple devices, consider renting a portable WiFi device (commonly called MiFi or a pocket WiFi). These nifty gadgets are about the size of a deck of cards and create your own personal Wi-Fi bubble wherever you go. Perfect for families, friend groups, or digital nomads, these devices typically let you connect 5-10 devices at once - so everyone's phones, tablets, and laptops can stay online without fighting over who gets to use the data!

You've got several ways to get your hands on one. Companies like TravelWiFi, Hippocket WiFi, and My Webspot specialize in tourist rentals and often have better rates than the big mobile carriers. You can book online before your trip and either pick up your device right at the airport (super convenient after a long flight!) or have it delivered to your hotel. Most rental companies offer unlimited data plans starting around £5-8 per day, which can be cheaper than getting separate SIM cards for everyone in your group. Plus, you'll only have to keep one device charged instead of managing multiple SIM cards.

Just keep in mind that while these devices are really convenient, their batteries usually last about 6-8 hours of active use, so you might want to pack a portable charger if you're planning long days of sightseeing. Many rental services provide spare batteries or car chargers if you need them. They also usually come with simple instructions in English and 24/7 customer support - really handy if you run into any technical hiccups during your trip. When your trip's over, most companies provide a prepaid envelope so you can just pop it in any Royal Mail post box before heading home!

Postal Services and Sending Items Home

Planning to send postcards to loved ones or mail home some goodies after a shopping spree? The UK's postal services make it a breeze.

The Royal Mail

The Royal Mail is the UK's national postal service and is known for its reliability and efficiency. You'll find post offices in towns, cities, and even tiny villages, and they're usually open from 9 a.m. to 5:30 p.m., Monday through Friday (with shorter hours on Saturdays).

For postcards and letters, look for the iconic red postboxes scattered across the UK. Stamps are available at post offices, supermarkets, and even convenience stores. If you want your letter to get there faster, opt for 1st Class service within the UK or an international service for overseas mail (*Royal Mail and Parcelforce Worldwide UK Services*). Be aware though, the cost to send a 1st Class letter or postcard from the UK to the US is currently about £2.80.

Sending Parcels Home

Bought too many souvenirs? No problem! The Royal Mail also handles parcels of all sizes. You can choose from a variety of shipping options, from standard services to premium tracked and signed-for delivery. For extra peace of mind, use a service with tracking so you can monitor your package's journey.

For particularly heavy or valuable items, consider private courier companies like DHL, FedEx, or UPS. These services can often provide faster shipping and additional security for high-value packages. Many couriers have convenient drop-off locations in major cities and even offer free packing materials.

Customs Reminders

Remember to check your home country's customs rules before shipping items. Some products, like alcohol, certain foods, or plant materials, may be restricted. Better safe than sorry!

Shipping From Shops

If you've purchased something large—like antiques or artwork—many UK retailers offer international shipping. Ask the store staff about their shipping options, costs, and expected delivery times.

Tips for Staying Connected While Traveling

Let's not forget about the practical tips for staying connected while navigating the UK:

- **Download useful apps:** Apps like Google Maps, Citymapper, and Rome2rio can help you find attractions, plan routes and navigate public transport. For communication, WhatsApp, Skype, and Zoom are excellent options for staying in touch with your family and friends.

- **Pack a power bank:** If you're out and about all day, your phone battery might run low quickly (especially if you're snapping pictures or using GPS). A portable power bank can save the day and keep your devices charged throughout.

- **Check your device compatibility**: If you're bringing electronics from home, make sure they are compatible with UK electrical standards (230V). Some devices may need a voltage converter in addition to a plug adapter.

- **Leverage virtual numbers:** If you need a temporary, reliable UK number for business or emergencies, consider virtual services like Google Voice or Skype. These let you make and receive calls over Wi-Fi without needing a local SIM card.

The UK makes it easy to stay connected, whether you're using a local SIM card, logging into free Wi-Fi hotspots, or even mailing postcards to loved ones back home. When you plan ahead, you can avoid unexpected charges, enjoy reliable internet access, and ensure your phone is ready to capture every magical moment of your trip.

Now go ahead and share those travel updates, call your family, and keep those maps loaded—you've got everything you need to stay connected and make the most of your UK adventure!

Chapter Seven

Electrical Appliances and Connectivity

When you're packing for your UK trip, it's easy to overlook one critical question: "Will my gadgets work there?" Electrical appliances, plugs, and connectivity are some of those often-forgotten travel essentials that can either make your trip smooth or leave you scrambling at the last minute. The UK's electrical system is different from many other countries, and understanding how to stay plugged in (literally!) will save you a lot of frustration. Therefore, worry not! In this chapter, we will take you through everything you need to know about powering up in the UK, including electrical standards, adapters, converters, and even purchasing electronics while you're in the UK.

UK Electrical Standards and Plug Types

The UK has unique electrical safety standards, which means you can expect high-quality outlets and appliances. Here's what you need to know:

Switches on Outlets

Many UK electrical outlets often have individual on/off switches. You'll need to flip the switch to turn on the power to the outlet/socket, which can take some getting used to. However, this is great for saving energy and preventing accidental shocks.

Fused Plugs

UK plugs include a built-in fuse, which protects against electrical surges. This adds an extra layer of safety, but it also means the plugs are bulkier than those in many other countries.

Extension Cords and Power Strips

If you're traveling with multiple devices, consider bringing a power strip that works with your adapter for convenience. Also, you can look for one with built-in surge protection for added safety.

Voltage and Frequency

In the UK, electricity runs on 230 volts at a frequency of 50 Hz. If you're visiting from countries like the US, Canada, or another country where the voltage is typically 100–120 volts, you'll need to check whether your devices are dual voltage. Dual voltage appliances can handle both 110V and 230V, making them travel-friendly.

If your device isn't dual voltage, plugging it into a UK outlet without a voltage converter could fry it. And let's be honest—no one wants to explain to their boss why their work laptop smells like burnt plastic!

Plug Types

UK Electrical Plug

UK plugs use a distinctive Type G plug, which has three rectangular prongs arranged in a triangular shape. These plugs are larger and more robust than many other plug types in most countries and feature built-in fuses for added safety.

Travel tip: Unlike in some countries where you might be able to *force* a plug into an outlet (not recommended!), don't try to force your non-UK plugs into a UK socket—it won't fit, and you could damage your device or the outlet. Instead, you'll need an adapter or converter (more on that shortly!).

Buying and Using Adapters and Converters

When you're traveling internationally, adapters and converters are your best friends. Without them, you'll be left staring at a dead phone, a powerless laptop, and a useless electric toothbrush. Many people mix up adapters and converters, but they serve very different purposes. Here's a quick guide on what you need and how to use them without a hitch.

Adapters

Adapters are small devices that allow you to physically connect your device's plug to the UK's Type G socket. They don't change the voltage or frequency—they're just a bridge between your plug and the wall outlet.

If your devices are dual voltage (e.g., marked with *100-240V, 50/60Hz*), an adapter is all you'll need. Dual voltage devices automatically adjust to the local electrical standard, so you're good to go.

Adapters are lightweight, affordable, and easy to find online or at travel stores. Consider buying a universal adapter that works in multiple countries if you're planning to travel elsewhere in the future.

Converters

Converters go a step further by actually changing the voltage. This is essential if your device only works on 110 volts and isn't dual voltage.

Converters can be bulky and expensive, so it's often easier to leave high-power appliances like hair dryers, straighteners, or electric razors that aren't dual voltage at home and use the hotel's or buy a UK-compatible version.

Be cautious when using converters, as improper use can damage your devices. Always check the power requirements on your appliance before plugging it in.

To make things easier, here's a quick guide to what you'll need for different devices:

- **Smartphone/tablet:** adapter (most are dual voltage).

- **Laptop:** adapter (most are dual voltage).

- **Camera battery charger:** adapter (check if dual voltage).

- **Hair dryer and styling tools:** converter (if not dual voltage) or buy a UK-compatible version.

- **Electric razor/toothbrush:** adapter (check if dual voltage).

Travel tip: Some travel adapters come with USB ports, so you can charge multiple devices at once—handy for phones, tablets, and other gadgets! Additionally, mark your adapters and converters with a label or sticker so you don't mix them up. Using the wrong one could damage your device!

With a bit of preparation, keeping your devices connected and charged in the UK is a walk in the park! Just pack your adapters, check your voltage requirements, and plan your electronics purchases ahead of time. Now you're ready to stay connected, charged up, and stress-free as you explore everything the UK has to offer!

Chapter Eight

Where to Stay?

Finding the perfect place to stay is a big part of making your UK trip unforgettable. Whether you're dreaming of staying in a cozy countryside B&B, a chic London hotel, or a budget-friendly hostel, there's something for everyone. But be warned: Accommodation in the UK isn't always what you might expect if you're used to American standards. Don't worry—we've got all the insider tips and tricks to help you choose the right spot for your stay.

Types of Accommodation: Hotels, B&Bs, Hostels, and Short-Term Rentals

The UK has a variety of accommodations to suit every style and budget. Whether you're looking for historical charm, modern convenience, or budget-friendly comfort, here are the main options: From cozy bed & breakfasts tucked away in centuries-old cottages to sleek city-center hotels with panoramic views, each type of stay offers its own unique slice of British hospitality.

Hotels

Fancy a hotel? British hotels are just as varied as the country itself! From modern city skyscrapers to boutique hotels in buildings older than America (yes, really), there's no shortage of charm. That said, hotel rooms in the UK tend to be smaller than their American counterparts, and finding two full-sized beds in a room to accommodate four people is much trickier. If you need two beds, chains like Premier Inn or Travelodge are a safe bet, but always double-check before booking. The good news? Many UK hotels are housed in stunning period buildings, so you might get to sleep in a Tudor mansion or a Georgian townhouse. How's that for a story to tell your friends?

Bed and Breakfasts (B&Bs)

Country Cottage

Staying at a B&B is the ultimate way to soak up British hospitality. These are often run by friendly locals, and you'll feel right at home as you sip tea and chat with your hosts. Oh, and let's not forget the main event: the legendary full English breakfast. We're talking eggs, sausages, baked beans, and even black pudding if you're feeling adventurous. B&Bs are perfect for small towns and rural escapes, where you'll wake up to the sound of birds chirping and maybe even a view of rolling green hills.

Unlike larger hotels, each B&B has its own unique character - you might find yourself in a cozy Victorian townhouse, a converted farmhouse, or a charming cottage with a garden full of roses. Many B&B owners take pride in preserving historic features while adding modern comforts like ensuite bathrooms and reliable Wi-Fi. The best part is the personal touch: your hosts can point you toward hidden local gems like that perfect village pub or a scenic walking trail that doesn't show up in guidebooks. And if you're traveling during peak season (especially summer months or around local festivals), book well in advance - the most charming B&Bs often fill up months ahead, particularly in popular areas like the Cotswolds or the Lake District.

Hostels

If you're on a budget, hostels are an excellent option. The Youth Hostels Association (YHA) operates many affordable and comfortable hostels across the UK, often in scenic locations like national parks or coastal areas. Hostels typically provide dormitory-style accommodation, but private rooms are often available at an additional cost. They're also a great way to meet fellow travelers, particularly for solo adventurers.

Most UK hostels have come a long way from the bare-bones accommodations of the past - nowadays you'll often find well-equipped self-catering kitchens, comfortable common rooms with free Wi-Fi, and helpful staff who can recommend local attractions and activities. Some YHA properties are absolutely stunning, housed in converted castles, Victorian mansions, or historic buildings with fascinating stories to tell. And don't worry if you're not exactly a "youth" anymore - despite the name, these hostels welcome travelers of all ages who are looking for an affordable accommodation with a social atmosphere.

Short-Term Rentals

Platforms like Airbnb, Vrbo and HolidayCottages.co.uk offer a wide range of short-term rentals, from chic city apartments to cozy countryside cottages. Rentals are ideal for families or groups, as they often come with amenities like full kitchens, making it easier to save on meals. However, rural properties may require a car for convenience, so plan accordingly. Keep in mind that short-term rentals are subject to availability and may have strict cancellation policies.

One of the best parts about staying in a rental is that you can really live like a local - imagine waking up in a converted barn in the Yorkshire Dales, or cooking breakfast in your own flat just steps from Edinburgh's Royal Mile! Many hosts go above and beyond to make your stay special, often leaving thoughtful welcome baskets with local treats or detailed guides to their favorite neighborhood spots. When booking, pay special attention to the reviews, particularly comments about the location and the host's responsiveness - a great host can make all the difference in your experience. And here's a pro tip: if you're booking a city rental, look for properties near public transport links (especially in London), as this can save you tons of time and money on getting around. Just remember that in historic buildings (which many UK rentals are), you might encounter quirky features like narrow staircases, no elevators or low ceilings - all part of the charm of staying in a piece of British history!

Booking Tips and Recommendations

Ready to book your accommodation? Here are some practical tips to make sure you snag the best spot:

1. **Book early:** Popular spots fill up quickly, especially during peak times like summer or big events (think Wimbledon or the Edinburgh Fringe Festival). Book several months in advance to get the best deals and availability. This is particularly true for smaller towns during their famous local events - like Hay-on-Wye during the Literary Festival in May, or the Lake District during the summer walking season. Even seemingly quiet areas can get surprisingly busy during bank holiday weekends!

2. **Location:** In cities, try to stay near public transportation, like a Tube or train station—it'll save you tons of time and effort. In rural areas, pick accommodations close to the landmarks or activities you're planning to explore. For London specifically, look for places in Zone 1 or 2 on the Tube map to keep your travel times manageable. In Edinburgh, staying near Waverley Station puts you right in the heart of both the Old and New Towns, while still giving you easy access to day trips.

3. **Check for amenities:** British accommodations can be a little different from what you're used to. Mini-fridges aren't always a given, but you'll almost always find tea and coffee-making facilities. Air conditioning? Rare in older buildings, especially outside major cities, so if you're visiting in the warmer months (July or August), confirm that your room has it. Also, don't be surprised if your room has separate hot and cold water taps in older buildings - it's just one of those charming British quirks! And while most places now offer free Wi-Fi, speeds can vary dramatically in rural areas, so check recent reviews if staying connected is important to you.

4. **Read reviews:** Take the time to read guest reviews on sites like TripAdvisor, Booking.com, or Airbnb. Honest feedback from fellow travelers is worth its weight in gold and can save you from unwelcome surprises. Pay special attention to comments about noise levels - many charming

historic pubs also offer rooms, but the trade-off might be some evening revelry from below. Similarly, those lovely period properties in city centers might mean you'll hear the morning hustle and bustle of delivery trucks and street cleaners.

5. **Be flexible with cancellation:** Travel plans change, and life happens. Look for accommodations with free or flexible cancellation policies so you're not stuck in a sticky situation. This is especially important if you're planning to travel during the UK's notoriously unpredictable weather seasons - spring and autumn can be gorgeous, but they can also bring unexpected storms that might affect your plans. Many properties now offer reasonable cancellation policies thanks to lessons learned during the pandemic, but always read the fine print carefully. And invest in travel insurance.

Quirky and Unexpected Differences Between US and UK Accomodations

Let's talk about what to expect when you finally check in. Accommodations in the UK come with their quirks and charms. Here's the lowdown:

- Be prepared for cozy (read: small) rooms, especially in cities or historical buildings. If you're traveling as a family or group, you might want to look into short-term rentals for more space. Really look carefully at any photos provided to make sure you will have all the space you need.

- Many UK accommodations don't have air conditioning. Summers in the UK are usually mild (highs in the 70s F), but if you're visiting in July or August, double-check if A/C is available, especially in southern regions where it might get warmer. It is not unheard of to have temps above 90F in a heat wave, which are becoming more common.

- Another difference is in the way floors are numbered. In the UK, the ground floor is labeled "0," and the first floor is one floor up. So, when you press "1" on the elevator, you're heading up to the second level! This can be a bit of a mind-bender if you're used to the US system.

- And here's a delightful little perk—almost every hotel room, no matter how basic, will have tea and coffee-making facilities. Enjoy your morning cuppa, the British way!

- As for electrical outlets, UK bathrooms typically don't have regular ones for safety reasons (though there might be a special one for shavers). If you're planning to use a hairdryer or straightener, a cordless rechargeable version can come in handy. But don't worry—if you don't have a cordless option, you'll usually find plugs near a mirror somewhere else in the room, so you won't be left fumbling in the dark!

- In the UK, you often have to switch electric plugs "on" to use them (see the previous chapter). And speaking of electricity, in many hotels, you'll need to insert your room key into a slot near the door to activate the lights (Mavromatakis, 2019). No key, no lights! It's a small detail, but one to keep in mind so you aren't wondering why none of the lights work.

- Also, when it comes to light switches, they can be a little different in the UK. In most UK hotels, a light switch will typically be designed so that the "on" position is "down." Yes, that's right! You'll need to flick the switch downwards to turn the light on. This is the standard practice in the UK and other Commonwealth countries, unlike in the US where "on" is usually "up" on a toggle switch. A tiny detail that might take some getting used to, but you'll get the hang of it in no time!

- This one catches people off guard—the bathroom light switch is almost always outside the bathroom! It's a little quirk of British building design, so don't be surprised if you find yourself stepping back out of the bathroom to turn the lights on.

- Alternatively, you'll often find a pull cord for the light switch hanging from the ceiling instead of a regular switch - this is another safety feature due to electrical regulations. They can be surprisingly long and sometimes hide behind doors!

- Why does the toilet have flush options? Quaintly, toilets in the UK often have two buttons on the toilet, larger and smaller. While getting this wrong is hardly a big problem, just in case you were wondering, the little button is for a little flush for liquids, and the big button is for a more powerful flush. 'Nuff said.

- Many older hotels and B&Bs still have separate hot and cold water taps in bathrooms and sinks, rather than a single mixer tap. This dates back to old plumbing systems where hot water came from a storage tank and cold water came directly from the mains. While modern buildings typically have mixer taps, you might encounter these dual taps in charming historic properties.

- Electric shower units are common in UK bathrooms - these are wall-mounted units that heat the water as it flows through, rather than drawing from a central water heater. They might look a bit industrial compared to American shower fixtures, but they're perfectly normal in the UK. Just remember to turn on the power switch (usually with a pull cord) before expecting hot water!

- Here's something you never knew you needed – a British towel warmer! Look for the chrome or white ladder-style rail in your bathroom - it's either connected to the home's central heating system or runs by an electric switch, and warms up automatically. For the coziest results, fold your towel in half lengthwise and drape it over multiple rungs. And a local secret - try warming your pajamas too! Just remember a quick touch test first, as they can get quite hot. It's one of those charming British comforts you'll wish you had back home!

- In many older buildings, you might find radiators instead of central heating vents. These often have individual controls, so you can adjust the temperature in your room. During summer they're usually turned off, but in spring and autumn, you might want to know how to operate them for chilly evenings.

- Window designs might surprise you - most UK buildings have casement windows that swing outward using a crank handle or push-out mechanism. These windows often have multiple positions for ventilation, from just cracked open to fully extended. You'll usually find a little handle or latch that locks them in your desired position, which is handy for those breezy British days! Some even come with a special security setting that lets you leave them slightly open for fresh air while keeping things secure. Just remember to close them properly when it rains (which, let's be honest, happens quite a bit in the UK!).

- Unlike in America, British windows typically come without screens.

This isn't an oversight—the UK's milder climate means fewer mosquitoes and biting insects make screens unnecessary! While this enhances airflow and architectural charm, families with small children should be mindful of this safety consideration, especially in upper-floor accommodations.

- If you're staying in a short-term rental, you might encounter a "combi boiler" for hot water and heating. These need to be switched on to get hot water (unlike American systems that keep a tank hot all the time). Your host should explain how to use it, but it's worth asking if you're not familiar with them.

- While Americans are used to ice machines in hotel corridors, these are rare in UK hotels. If you need ice, you'll usually need to request it from the bar or reception. Similarly, vending machines for snacks and drinks are less common - though many hotels offer room service or have a small shop in the lobby.

- If you're staying somewhere with laundry facilities, don't be surprised to find a single washer/dryer combo unit rather than separate machines - these are super common in the UK where space is often tight! These combination machines tend to wash beautifully but dry much slower than Americans are used to, so plan ahead and expect a full dry cycle to take 2-3 hours for a small load. Many Brits actually skip the dryer function altogether and use a drying rack (which you'll often find provided). Keep this in mind while packing and opt for quick-drying fabrics.

Choosing the Right Accommodation

So, how do you decide where to stay? Here's a quick rundown to help you choose:

- **Hotels:** Ideal if you're looking for convenience and modern amenities. Great for city stays or business trips. Most UK hotels, even budget chains like Premier Inn and Travelodge, maintain reliable standards and often include a proper full English breakfast in your room rate.

- **B&Bs:** Perfect for travelers who love a cozy, personalized experience and a good home-cooked breakfast. These family-run establishments often occupy charming period buildings and can offer incredible value for money, especially in popular tourist areas like the Cotswolds or Lake District where hotels tend to be pricier.

- **Hostels:** The best option for budget travelers or anyone looking to meet new people. Many UK hostels, particularly those run by the YHA, are located in fascinating historic buildings - you might find yourself staying in a converted castle, lighthouse, or Victorian mansion!

- **Short-term rentals:** Fantastic for families, groups, or long-term stays, with the added bonus of homey comforts like kitchens. In rural areas, you might luck out with a truly unique property like a converted shepherd's hut, traditional cottage with a thatched roof, or even a restored windmill turned holiday home.

- **Speciality rentals:** Did you know you can even rent entire manor homes or cottages that are situated on private estates? Your host may even be a member of nobility! Yes, for real! My personal favorite – Mapperton Estate in South West England in Dorset, run by the Earl and Countess of Sandwich, Luke and Julie Montagu. Visit mapperton.com.

The best choice will depend on your travel style, group size, and budget. However, wherever you stay, you'll experience the warm hospitality the UK is famous for. After all, a cozy bed and a good night's sleep make all the difference when you're out exploring!

Chapter Nine

Eating Out and British Cuisine

When it comes to food, the UK is packed with surprises—think hearty comfort meals, quirky dining customs, and a love affair with tea and pubs. British dining is a feast for the senses (and your Instagram!), so let's dive into everything you need to know about enjoying the local flavors, navigating restaurant etiquette, and embracing pub culture.

Ready? Grab your appetite, and let's go!

Overview of British Cuisine

British cuisine has come a long way from its reputation of being "bland." Today, it's a delightful mix of traditional dishes, modern innovations, and global influences. Classic British food is all about warmth and comfort. Think flaky pies filled with tender meat and gravy, crispy roast potatoes alongside succulent beef, and golden fish and chips by the seaside. Hungry yet?

Breakfast is also a big deal here, and nothing beats a full English breakfast—it's practically a rite of passage! For those with a sweet tooth, British desserts like sticky toffee pudding or scones with clotted cream and jam are absolute must-tries.

But the UK isn't stuck in its traditional ways. The culinary scene has embraced flavors from around the world, with Indian curries, Caribbean jerk chicken, and even Japanese sushi popping up in every major city. So, whether you're a foodie or just love a good meal, Britain's got you covered.

Food Favorites By Another Name

Looking for some comfortable favorites? Here are some American foods and their UK counterparts - think of this as your "translation guide" to British grocery shopping! Sometimes the differences are subtle (like slightly different names), and sometimes they're quite different products entirely. But don't worry - you can usually find something similar to what you're craving, even if it goes by a different name.

- What Americans call "baked potatoes" or "stuffed potatoes" are called "jacket potatoes" in the UK (and they're a very popular lunch option, often filled with baked beans, cheese, tuna mayo, or chili)

- American "cookies" are generally called "biscuits" in the UK - though you'll see "cookie" used for the bigger, chunkier American-style ones. And remember, if a Brit mentions "scones," they're talking about something closer to an American "biscuit" but slightly sweeter

- American "french fries" are "chips" in Britain, while American "potato chips" are called "crisps." To make it more confusing, "steak fries" or "wedges" are often called "potato wedges" or "chunky chips"

- American "cotton candy" is called "candy floss," "eggplant" is "aubergine," "zucchini" is "courgette," and "cilantro" is always called "coriander"

- A "grilled cheese sandwich" in America is a "cheese toastie" in the UK, and it's often made in a special sealed toasting machine rather than in a pan

- What Americans call "ground beef" is called "minced beef" or just "mince" in the UK. So a "ground beef patty" would be a "beef mince patty" or just "beef burger"

- American "broiling" is called "grilling" in the UK, while American "grilling" (as in barbecue) is called "barbecuing"

- If you want "jelly" for your peanut butter sandwich, ask for "jam" - British "jelly" is what Americans call "Jell-O"

- American "heavy cream" is called "double cream," "half-and-half" is called "single cream," and "whipping cream" is well, called "whipping cream"

- Want ranch dressing? This very American condiment can be tricky to find! Look in the American food section of larger supermarkets, or try "garlic and herb" dressing for a similar taste. The same goes for American-style Italian dressing - the closest equivalent might be called "vinaigrette"

- You might be surprised when your bacon arrives! What Americans know as bacon (thin, crispy strips) is called "streaky bacon" in the UK, and it's not the most popular choice. British bacon, called "back bacon" or "rashers," is more like a small, round piece of ham with a strip of fat around the edge. It comes from the loin rather than the belly of the pig, making it leaner and meatier than American-style bacon. When Brits have a "bacon butty" (bacon sandwich) or a "full English breakfast," they're using this back bacon, which stays tender and juicy rather than getting crispy. If you're craving American-style bacon, just ask specifically for "streaky bacon"

Remember, these differences can sometimes lead to amusing misunderstandings - like if you ask for a "biscuit" expecting an American-style breakfast biscuit, you might end up with a cookie instead!

British Dining Etiquette and Tipping Culture

Dining in the UK comes with its own set of unspoken rules. Here's a quick rundown so you can avoid any awkward faux pas:

- In restaurants, it's common to wait to be seated by a host or server. If you're dining at a pub, it's usually self-service—find a table, check the menu, and then order at the bar.

- Brits typically use the European style of dining, where the fork is held in the left hand and the knife in the right. Don't worry if you're not used to it—no one will judge if you switch things up.

- Tipping isn't as big a deal as in the US. A service charge (usually 10-12%) is often added to your bill at restaurants, especially in cities. If it's not included, leaving a 10% tip is perfectly fine. At pubs, tipping isn't necessary, but you can round up to the nearest pound or buy the bartender a drink if you're feeling generous (Worsnop, 2019).

- If you've made a reservation, be on time. Brits value punctuality, and arriving late without notice is considered rude.

- The UK has a more subdued dining culture than some other countries, so keep conversations at a moderate volume.

- When you're finished with your meal, place your knife and fork parallel to each other at the "4:20" position on your plate (like clock hands), with the tines of the fork facing up. This is the universal signal to your server that you're done eating. If you're just taking a break, rest your cutlery in an inverted 'V' shape with the tips meeting in the center of the plate - this tells the server not to clear your plate just yet!

- Don't be surprised if your server doesn't check on you as frequently as they would in the US. British service tends to be more hands-off, letting you enjoy your meal in peace. If you need something, it's perfectly fine to catch your server's eye or raise your hand slightly - no need to wave frantically!

- "Pudding" is what the Brits often call dessert, and it doesn't necessarily mean an actual pudding. When someone asks if you'd like "afters" or the "pudding menu," they're talking about dessert options. And if you hear someone mention "spotted dick," try not to giggle - it's just a traditional steamed pudding with dried fruit!

- When dining in a group, Brits usually split the bill equally (they call this "going Dutch" or "splitting the bill"), rather than calculating exactly what each person had. If you're not comfortable with this, it's best to mention it early in the meal. Also, many restaurants, especially for larger groups, won't split the bill on multiple cards, so it's good to have cash handy or use a bill-splitting app.

- One big difference you'll notice is that meals in the UK tend to be more leisurely affairs. Unlike in the US, where you might feel pressured to eat and scoot, Brits often linger over their meals and no one will rush you out the door. It's completely normal to spend two or three hours at dinner, chatting between courses and staying at your table long after the plates are cleared. In fact, asking for the bill too quickly might be seen as a bit eager - servers will usually wait for you to signal that you're ready to leave. This is especially true in pubs where people often stay at their tables for hours, nursing drinks and enjoying conversation. Just don't expect the quick turnover you're used to in American restaurants - dinner out is seen as the entertainment for the evening, not just a pit stop before the next activity!

Must-Try British Foods and Traditional Pubs

No trip to the UK would be complete without sampling some classic British dishes. Here's what should be on your foodie bucket list:

- **Fish and chips:** A crispy, golden classic served with mushy peas and a squeeze of lemon. Head to a seaside town for the best version.

- **Sunday roast:** A traditional meal of roasted meat (like beef, lamb, or chicken), Yorkshire pudding, roast potatoes, and vegetables, all drenched in gravy.

- **Full English breakfast:** Eggs, bacon, sausages, baked beans, grilled tomatoes, black pudding, and toast. It's a hearty start to the day and a British institution.

- **Shepherd's pie:** A comforting dish of minced/chopped meat (traditionally lamb), vegetables like carrots and peas, topped with creamy mashed potatoes and baked until golden.

- **Sticky toffee pudding:** A dessert made of moist sponge cake, dates, and a rich toffee sauce. Perfect with a scoop of vanilla ice cream.

When it comes to drinks, the UK is famous for its pub culture. A visit to a traditional pub is a must, whether it's for a pint of beer, a cider, or even just a soft drink. Many pubs also serve excellent food, often referred to as "pub grub." Look out for hearty dishes like steak and ale pie or Ploughman's lunch.

Pub Culture

Pubs, short for "public houses," are much more than just spots for a drink—they're a key part of British social life and often the heart of local communities. Each pub has its unique vibe, from historic coaching inns with wooden beams and roaring fires to quirky modern hangouts filled with craft beer taps and artisanal spirits. Think of them as Britain's living rooms: places where locals gather to celebrate, commiserate, or just catch up over a pint.

Here are some tips to help you navigate the wonderful world of British pubs:

- Unlike in restaurants, at the pub you'll usually order your drinks and food at the bar, pay upfront, and carry your own drinks to the table. No waiting for a server to bring your bill! Just remember to make a mental note of your table number if you're ordering food.

- In a group, it's common to take turns buying rounds of drinks. Don't leave before it's your turn to buy! This tradition of "buying rounds" is deeply ingrained in pub culture. If you're not planning to stay long, it's perfectly fine to say "I'll get my own" at the start - just make that clear before the rounds begin.

- Many pubs are now "gastropubs," offering high-quality, creative dishes. It's not just about beer anymore—think artisan cocktails, carefully curated wine lists, and seasonal menus featuring local ingredients. Some gastropubs have even earned Michelin stars! Sunday roast at a good pub is a British institution - expect generous portions of roasted meat, crispy potatoes, Yorkshire puddings, and all the trimmings.

- Many pubs welcome children during the day and often have a special kids' menu. Just double-check the rules, as some may have age restrictions in the evenings. Family-friendly pubs might have outdoor play areas or games rooms, making them perfect for a relaxed family lunch.

- Each pub has its own personality and quirks. You might find one with a resident dog or cat, another famous for its quiz nights, or one that's supposedly haunted! Traditional pubs often have interesting names with historical significance - "The King's Arms," "The Red Lion," or "The Crown" usually date back to times when most people couldn't read and needed picture signs to identify the pub.

- Most pubs follow traditional opening hours, typically 11am to 11pm (though this varies). "Last orders" is usually announced by a bell about 20-30 minutes before closing time, giving you a chance to get one final drink in. After that, you'll hear the familiar call of "Time, ladies and gentlemen!" signaling it's time to finish up.

- Don't feel like you have to stick to beer - pubs serve all sorts of drinks. If you're not sure what to order, most bartenders (they're called "publicans" in traditional pubs) are happy to offer recommendations. British beer comes in various styles, from traditional "real ales" (served slightly warmer than American beer) to modern craft brews. And if you're not drinking alcohol, most pubs now offer a good selection of non-alcoholic options too.

- Many pubs serve as community hubs, hosting events like pub quizzes, live music nights, or local club meetings. If you're traveling solo, these can be great ways to meet locals and experience authentic British culture. Just remember that pub quizzes are taken very seriously - no googling answers on your phone!

British pubs are meant to be relaxed, friendly places. Don't worry too much about making a faux pas - as long as you're polite and respectful, you'll be welcomed like a regular. And if you're unsure about anything, just ask - Brits are usually happy to help visitors navigate their beloved pub culture!

Tea Time

Now, let's switch gears and talk about tea—because what's more British than having a cuppa? According to research, *Tea Time: Taste Your Tea according to the English Tradition* (2021), here are a few different types of tea experiences:

Scone with Cream and Jam

- **Afternoon tea:** This is a special treat served in the afternoon, usually between 3 p.m. and 5 p.m. It includes small sandwiches, scones with clotted cream and jam, and cakes or pastries, along with a pot of tea. It's a relaxing and fun way to take a break. Traditional afternoon tea is often served on a three-tiered stand, starting with savory items on the bottom, scones in the middle, and finishing with sweets on top. The sandwiches are typically dainty "finger sandwiches" with classic fillings like cucumber, smoked salmon, egg and cress, or coronation chicken. Many fancy hotels and tea rooms offer champagne afternoon tea for special occasions, and you'll often need to book in advance. Don't feel pressured to dress up in your finest clothes, but smart casual is appropriate - no flip-flops or beachwear!

- **High tea:** High tea is not as fancy as it sounds. It's more like a meal served in the early evening and includes things like pies, bread, and cold meats. It's filling and hearty. Historically, this was the working class evening meal, served when people came home from work around 5-6pm. The "high" refers to the fact that it was eaten at a high table (dining table) rather than low tea tables used for afternoon tea. You might find dishes like shepherd's pie, sausage rolls, baked beans on toast, or cold cuts with pickles. While less common nowadays, some traditional cafes and hotels still serve high tea, particularly in northern England and Scotland. It's basically an early dinner rather than the formal affair that tourists often imagine!

- **Cream tea:** Cream tea is a simple and delicious snack. You get scones, clotted cream, jam, and tea. It's very popular in places like Devon and Cornwall. This tradition sparked one of Britain's friendliest regional rivalries - Devon and Cornwall disagree on whether the cream or jam should go on the scone first! The Cornish method is jam first, then cream, while Devon insists on cream first, then jam. Clotted cream is unique to this part of Britain - it's thick, rich, and yellowish with a slightly crusty top, made by heating cream until it "clots." A proper cream tea should come with freshly baked scones (still slightly warm), strawberry jam, and generous portions of clotted cream. The tea served is usually English Breakfast or Earl Grey, though you can typically request other varieties. Be warned - once you've had proper clotted cream, regular whipped cream will never taste the same!

Whether you're enjoying a fancy afternoon tea, a hearty high tea, or a simple cream tea in a village café, taking time for this cherished British tradition is a delightful way to experience local culture. So put down your phone, pour a cuppa, and savor the moment!

Dietary Needs and Food Allergies

If you have dietary restrictions or food allergies, don't worry—the UK is well-equipped to cater to your needs. Most menus indicate common allergens like gluten, nuts, and dairy. Restaurants and cafés are required by law to provide allergen information, so don't hesitate to ask your server.

Vegetarians and vegans will feel right at home in the UK. Many restaurants and pubs now offer delicious plant-based options, and supermarkets are stocked with a variety of vegan products. Halal and kosher choices are also widely available, especially in larger cities.

If you're traveling with severe allergies, it's a good idea to carry an allergy card detailing your specific needs. While most staff in UK restaurants are well-trained to handle dietary requests, it's always better to be cautious. When in doubt, opt for chain restaurants or well-reviewed establishments with clear policies on food preparation. And remember to double-check ingredient lists or ask your server if you're unsure—most places are happy to accommodate!

Wrapping up your culinary adventure in the UK, it's clear that eating out is about much more than just the food—it's about savoring the culture, history, and traditions that make Britain so unique. From cozy pub meals to Michelin-starred dining, there's something to satisfy every craving and curiosity. Be open to trying new dishes, enjoy the charm of traditional pubs, and don't shy away from asking for recommendations—locals often know the hidden gems!

Bon appétit—or as the Brits might say, "Tuck in and enjoy!"

Chapter Ten

At the Grocery Store

Shopping for groceries in the UK is a fun little adventure, especially when you discover all the little differences. You'll find a mix of big supermarkets like Tesco, Sainsbury's, and Morrisons, where you can get fresh produce and pantry staples. For travelers on a budget, discount favorites like Aldi and Lidl are a fantastic option, offering great value for money without sacrificing quality.

One standout feature of UK supermarkets is the wide selection of ready-made meals and snacks, which are surprisingly tasty, fresh, and convenient. Whether you're a solo traveler or a family on the go, these can be a lifesaver. For something simple, look for roast chicken portions, pasta dishes, or salads. Many stores also offer family-sized options like cottage pie, lasagna, or even Sunday roast-inspired meals.

Unlike in the US where ready meals are often seen as budget options, UK supermarket prepared foods are considered high-quality alternatives to cooking from scratch, with chains like Marks & Spencer and Waitrose particularly known for their premium ready meals (like sushi platters and quiches). And here's a local tip: most supermarkets drastically reduce the prices of their fresh ready meals in the evening (usually marked with yellow stickers), so if you're flexible about what you eat, shopping later in the day can save you quite a bit of money!

Traveling with children? Supermarkets in the UK have you covered with kid-friendly options like mini pizzas, chicken goujons (tenders), and pre-packed lunches. This can be a huge help for families trying to keep everyone fed and happy while on the move. And if you're looking for something that feels a bit more special than standard kid's fare, check out the children's versions of traditional British dishes like shepherd's pie or fish pie, which come in smaller portions and are usually designed to be less spicy than adult versions!

And don't forget the meal deals—a sandwich, snack, and drink combo available at stores like Tesco or Sainsbury's for a budget-friendly price. They're perfect for a quick, affordable lunch or to pack for a day of sightseeing. While the sandwich selection might surprise Americans (prawn mayonnaise and cheese & pickle are local favorites!), you'll find the variety and value hard to beat, especially in expensive tourist areas where restaurant prices can be steep.

Where Are the Eggs? and Other Important Tips about Food

Here's a heads-up for Americans—don't expect to find eggs in the refrigerated section. In the UK, eggs are typically stored at room temperature. Why? British eggs are treated differently than American ones during production, so refrigeration isn't necessary for safety. Don't worry, they are perfectly safe and delicious!

- Get ready for new crisp (potato chip) flavors you've never imagined - prawn cocktail, pickled onion, and roast chicken are everyday favorites. And don't be confused if you see "Worcester Sauce" flavored crisps - they're a beloved British classic!

- Milk comes with different colored caps indicating the fat content, but not in the way Americans expect. Blue cap is whole milk, green is semi-skimmed (2%), and red is skimmed (fat-free) - the opposite of many US stores. You'll also find lots of UHT (shelf-stable) milk that doesn't need refrigeration until opened.

- The produce section might throw you off - vegetables are often sold by the piece rather than by weight (like "4 apples for £1"), and you'll find familiar vegetables with different names: zucchini is "courgette," eggplant is "aubergine," and arugula is "rocket."

- Looking for cilantro? Ask for "fresh coriander." Want heavy cream? Look for "double cream." And if a recipe calls for "cornflour," that's cornstarch in American terms. Looking for molasses? Ask for "treacle." Need confectioner's sugar? Look for "icing sugar." And if you're hunting for garbanzo beans, they're called "chickpeas" here. Looking to make some grits? You'll want to search for "polenta." And if a recipe calls for "spring onions," those are what Americans know as scallions.

- You won't find grape jelly, but you'll discover a world of interesting spreads like Marmite (a savory yeast extract spread), lemon curd, and various "fruit curds." The jam selection will introduce you to flavors like gooseberry and blackcurrant, which are rare in the US.

- Ready meals (TV dinners) are generally of much higher quality than in the US, and you'll find them everywhere - from Indian curry to shepherd's pie. They're not considered "budget food" but rather convenient options for busy people.

- In the bread aisle, you might be surprised to find chocolate-filled breakfast rolls (pain au chocolat) and other European-style pastries right alongside the regular bread, as well as an entire section dedicated to "digestive biscuits" - don't worry, they're just sweet wholemeal cookies, perfect for having with tea!

- You'll notice some uniquely British bread options too - crumpets (griddle cakes full of tiny holes perfect for soaking up butter), English muffins (different from American ones, with a drier, chewier texture), soft white "batch" rolls, crusty "tiger bread" (with its distinctive crackled crust), and sturdy "bloomer" loaves. And if you spot something called a "bap," that's just a soft round roll perfect for bacon sandwiches!

- The candy (or "sweets") aisle is a whole new world - Cadbury everything, Wine Gums (which contain no wine), Jelly Babies, and something called "dolly mixture." And chocolate bars taste different because UK chocolate typically has a higher milk content than American chocolate. Even familiar brands like Kit Kat, Milky Way, and Snickers taste noticeably different due to different recipes and ingredients - for example, UK Mars bars are closer to American Milky Ways, while a British Milky Way is more like a Three Musketeers bar!

- You'll also discover uniquely British treats like Maltesers (similar to Whoppers but meltier), Aero bars (chocolate full of tiny bubbles), Flake bars (crumbly rippled chocolate), and Turkish Delight - and while you might recognize some Cadbury products, there are dozens of varieties you've never seen in the US, from Curly Wurly (twisted chocolate-covered caramel) to Crunchie (honeycomb covered in chocolate).

Shopping in the UK is more than just filling your basket - it's a delightful journey through British culture and traditions! Whether you're hunting for colorful packets of uniquely British snacks, wandering through centuries-old market halls, or figuring out the charming quirks of local grocery stores, every shopping trip brings new discoveries. Take your time exploring these distinctly British retail experiences, embrace the wonderful differences you'll encounter, and savor all those marvelous little details that make shopping in the UK feel like a proper adventure all its own. And don't forget to keep your shopping bags handy - those 5p carrier bag charges at supermarkets are just another delightful part of embracing the local way of life!

Why Does This Soda Tastes Weird?

One thing that often surprises American visitors is how different sodas taste in the UK - and there's a good reason for that! Since 2018, the UK has had a "Sugar Tax" that encouraged drink manufacturers to reduce sugar content. Instead of creating separate diet and regular versions like in the US, many UK soft drinks now use a blend of regular sugar and artificial sweeteners, even in their "regular" versions. This means the line between "diet" and "regular" sodas is much more blurred than Americans are used to.

For example, regular Coca-Cola in the UK still has its original recipe (and pays the sugar tax), but Fanta, Sprite, and many other popular sodas have been reformulated with less sugar and added artificial sweeteners - even though they're not marketed as "diet" or "zero" versions. The labels will list sweeteners like aspartame or sucralose in the ingredients, but the front of the bottle might not mention it at all. If you're sensitive to artificial sweeteners or just prefer full-sugar sodas, you'll want to check the ingredients carefully. Some Americans say these reformulated drinks taste more like diet versions than what they're used to back home.

This can be particularly confusing when ordering at restaurants or pubs - what you think is "regular" soda might actually be the lower-sugar version with artificial sweeteners. If you're particular about your sodas, you might want to ask specifically for "full sugar" versions or check the ingredients on the bottle.

Another thing that might catch you off guard - "lemonade" in the UK isn't the traditional still, tart, freshly-squeezed lemon drink that Americans expect. Instead, when Brits say "lemonade," they're referring to a clear, carbonated lemon-lime soda (similar to Sprite or 7-Up). The traditional American-style lemonade does exist in the UK, but it's usually called "still lemonade" or "cloudy lemonade" to distinguish it from the fizzy kind. This is particularly important to know when ordering drinks like a "shandy" (beer mixed with lemonade) or cocktails - they'll always use the fizzy version. If you're craving that classic American-style lemonade, just ask for "cloudy" or "still" lemonade!

Just Some Water Please

When you ask for water at a restaurant or pub in Britain, your server will likely respond with "Still or sparkling?" - this isn't them being fancy, it's just the normal way to distinguish between flat water ("still") and carbonated mineral water ("sparkling" or sometimes called "fizzy"). While tap water is always free and perfectly safe to drink in the UK, you'll need to specifically ask for "tap water" if that's what you want, otherwise they'll assume you're ordering bottled water which comes with a charge. And here's a money-saving tip: some restaurants might try to steer you toward bottled water, but they're legally required to provide tap water if you ask for it!

Shopping for food in the UK isn't just about filling your grocery bag - it's a chance to experience British culture through its unique snacks, surprising flavors, and everyday essentials. Whether you're hunting for the perfect meal deal, discovering why HP Sauce (that mysterious brown condiment you'll see everywhere) is so beloved on bacon sandwiches, or trying to figure out the difference between digestive biscuits and regular cookies, every shopping trip is an adventure that helps you understand a little bit more about daily life in Britain.

Chapter Eleven

Shopping in the UK

Shopping in the UK is more than just a necessity; it's an experience. From charming high streets lined with boutique shops to bustling markets and sprawling shopping centers, there's something here for everyone. But if you're visiting from the US, there are a few quirks and differences you should know to make your retail adventures smooth and fun. So grab your bags (or a "trolley," as the Brits call it), and let's dive into the world of UK shopping!

High Streets, Markets, and Shopping Centers

One of the best things about shopping in the UK is the diversity of shopping environments. The high street is the heart of most British towns, lined with everything from big-name brands to quaint local stores. You'll find popular retailers like Marks & Spencer (famous for food, fashion, and their amazing meal deals), Boots (the go-to for toiletries and pharmacy items), Primark (budget-friendly fashion heaven), and WHSmith (great for books, magazines, and travel accessories). High streets are a great place to soak in local culture while picking up everyday essentials or gifts.

For a more unique experience, head to the markets. Borough Market in London is a foodie's paradise with artisanal cheeses, freshly baked bread, and mouth-watering street food. Portobello Road Market, also in London, is famous for its antiques and vintage finds, and in Camden Market, you'll find quirky fashion, handmade jewelry, and vintage goods. Across the UK, smaller towns often host weekly markets where locals sell fresh flowers, crafts, and baked goods. Markets are not only a fun place to shop but also an excellent spot for people-watching.

Prefer the convenience of a one-stop shop? British shopping centers (aka malls) are massive and loaded with options. Westfield London is one of the largest shopping centers in Europe, with everything from luxury designer brands to casual high-street fashion. Up north, Manchester's Trafford Centre combines shopping with entertainment, offering cinemas, restaurants, and even mini-golf. Shopping centers are perfect for rainy UK days when you need indoor fun (and let's be honest, the UK has plenty of those!).

Souvenirs and Unique British Products

When you're shopping for souvenirs in the UK, there are lots of great options to bring home a little piece of British culture. Here are some ideas for gifts and keepsakes, along with a few important tips on what you can and can't bring back with you:

For tea lovers, you can never go wrong with classic British tea. Pick up a box of Twinings or Yorkshire Tea to enjoy at home. If you want something a bit more special, go for a tin of Fortnum & Mason specialty tea or biscuits. These are beautifully packaged and very British!

Sweet treats also make fantastic gifts (or snacks for yourself!). You can't visit the UK without trying shortbread biscuits, and Walkers is a well-known brand. For chocolate lovers, Cadbury is a classic choice; you'll find everything from bars to boxed chocolates. Don't forget about marmalade, especially if you're a fan of Paddington Bear! It's perfect for your breakfast toast. If you're feeling adventurous, try Marmite. It's a strong, salty spread that has a passionate fan base. Some people love it, while others don't, but it's definitely something that sparks conversation!

And, of course, you'll want to grab a few Union Jack-themed souvenirs, whether it's a tote bag, mug, or even socks. If you're visiting Scotland, be sure to check out cashmere scarves, tartan handbags or whisky (Scotch)—iconic Scottish specialties.

But before you load up your suitcase with goodies, there are a few practical things to keep in mind:

- **No produce or plant materials:** You can't bring fresh fruits, vegetables, or plants into most countries, including the US. So leave the apples and flowers behind and go for something that's already packaged.

- **Limited alcohol:** If you're bringing back some liquor, like a bottle of Scotch whisky, there are some restrictions. The US allows you to bring in one liter of alcohol duty-free for personal use if you're 21 or older. If you're bringing more, you'll need to declare it at customs, and you'll likely have to pay duty taxes on it. The most important thing to note is that any alcohol you're carrying must be in your checked luggage (not carry-on) and should be well-protected—you don't want it breaking in transit! Also, it's always a good idea to check your specific airline's rules and the most current US Customs guidelines to ensure you're following the law.

- **Shipping larger items:** If you want to bring back something big, like an antique or large furniture piece, ask the shop if they offer shipping services. Many stores, especially antiques shops, will help arrange shipping to your home. This can be a great option if you fall in love with a unique item but don't want to deal with carrying it yourself. Keep in mind that shipping large items can be pricey, so check the cost before you commit!

So, whether you're picking up something small like a tea tin or planning to ship home a big find, there's no shortage of amazing British products to bring home. Just remember to check with your local customs about what you can legally bring back, so you won't be caught off guard at the airport!

Understanding VAT

There is no sales tax in the UK – they instead have a Value Added Tax (VAT) that is already included in the price of the item. So no surprises at the till!

Stores You Will Recognize by Another Name

Burger King, McDonald's, and Starbucks are everywhere, so you'll feel right at home. However, some stores you know and love in the US might go by a different name in the UK, which can be both fun and a little confusing (*American Shop Equivalents in the UK - Target, Pottery Barn & More*, 2024). For example:

TK Maxx

Yes, you read that right—it's not *TJ Maxx*, but *TK Maxx* in the UK. Despite the name change, it's the same treasure hunt experience for discounted designer goods and bargain deals, just with a slightly different sign. You can find everything from clothing to homeware, and half the fun is in the hunt for a great deal.

ASDA (Not Walmart)

If you're looking for a Walmart, you won't find one, but you will find ASDA, which is owned by Walmart and has a similar feel. It's a great place to shop for groceries, clothing, and household essentials, and you might even spot a few familiar brands while you're there (*American Shop Equivalents in the UK - Target, Pottery Barn & More*, 2024).

Sorry, No Targets!

Unfortunately, there are no Target stores in the UK, so if you're on the hunt for that mid-priced department store feel, you'll need to try something different. For a similar shopping experience, check out Marks & Spencer (known for high-quality food, clothing, and home goods), John Lewis (a more upscale department store with everything from electronics to fashion), or Debenhams (which has a mix of affordable and premium brands). If you're looking for budget-friendly options, Primark is a hugely popular choice for low-cost fashion and homeware. While it's not quite Target, it can still scratch that shopping itch!

Shopping Payments, Hours and Etiquette

Payment Methods in the UK

British payment systems might throw you off at first. Contactless payment is everywhere, with most places accepting tap-to-pay for purchases up to £100. Credit cards work differently too - you'll need a card with a chip, and you'll be asked to enter your PIN rather than sign. Be aware that American Express isn't as widely accepted as it is in the US, so it's good to have a Visa or Mastercard as back-up. Mobile payments like Apple Pay and Google Pay are extremely common and often don't have the same contactless limits as cards. One surprising difference? Personal checks (or "cheques" as they're spelled here) are rarely accepted in shops anymore. Most smaller shops prefer card or mobile payments, though they'll still take cash.

Understanding UK Store Hours

Don't expect the 24/7 shopping you might be used to in America. Most UK shops operate on shorter hours, typically opening around 9am and closing between 5:30-6pm on weekdays and Saturdays. Sundays are especially different - large stores can only open for six hours between 10am and 6pm (usually 10:30am-4:30pm or 11am-5pm) due to trading laws, though smaller shops can open longer. Bank holidays (public holidays) also affect shopping hours, with some stores closed completely or operating on Sunday hours. If you're planning a shopping trip, especially on Sundays or holidays, always check opening times in advance. Many stores also have a half-day during the week (often Wednesday or Thursday) when they close earlier than usual.

British Shopping Etiquette

Shopping etiquette in the UK is notably different from the US. First and foremost, queuing (standing in line) is taken very seriously - always join the back of any line and wait your turn. British shop assistants tend to be more reserved than their American counterparts; they'll help when asked but generally won't follow you around the store or make unsolicited suggestions. If you need assistance, a polite "Excuse me, please" is the way to go - avoid calling out "Hey!" or trying to get attention from across the store. When you hear "Are you being served?" it's a shop assistant asking if you're being helped. Also, the British consider it rude to touch or handle items excessively while shopping, so try to be mindful of this. And while friendly chat with shop staff is fine, the lengthy, personal conversations common in American stores aren't the norm here.

These cultural differences in shopping may seem small, but understanding them can make your UK shopping experience much more enjoyable and help you feel more like a local than a tourist!

In the end, remember shopping in the UK isn't just about buying things—it's about experiencing a different retail culture. While you might miss some of your favorite American stores, embrace the chance to explore uniquely British shops and discover new favorites. From the cheerful chaos of local markets to the refined elegance of department stores like Harrods, each shopping experience adds to your British adventure. And don't forget to save some space in your suitcase for those distinctly British treasures you won't find back home. Happy shopping!

Chapter Twelve

Health and Medical Care

Traveling is all about creating unforgettable memories, but nobody wants their grand adventure to be disrupted by unexpected health issues. Fortunately, the UK has a strong healthcare system and plenty of resources to keep you well and worry-free. Whether it's a little sniffle or a more serious emergency, knowing how to access medical care while you're abroad can save you precious time, reduce stress, and even keep a few more pounds in your pocket (the currency, not the weight!).

Now, get ready to embark on a journey through everything you need to know about staying healthy and handling medical needs during your UK adventure.

Understanding the National Health Service (NHS)

First things first—let's talk about the National Health Service (NHS). The NHS is the publicly funded healthcare system in the UK and a true British institution (Chang et al., n.d.). It provides free or low-cost healthcare to UK residents, but tourists can also benefit from its services. For visitors, if you happen to need urgent care or treatment during your stay, NHS hospitals and clinics will treat you, though some services may come with a fee.

The NHS is known for its accessibility and excellent care, though it can be a bit slower than private options due to its popularity and high demand. So, if you need non-urgent care or prefer quicker treatment, private healthcare is also available (we'll get to that shortly). Rest assured, if you're in a medical pinch, you'll be in good hands.

Here's the important bit for tourists: Emergency medical care is available to everyone, regardless of nationality, and hospitals will treat you even if you're not a UK resident. That said, non-residents will typically be billed for their care, so having medical travel insurance is a must.

How to Access Medical Care as a Tourist

If you feel unwell or need medical assistance during your trip, don't panic—help is readily available. Here's what you need to know:

- If you're facing a life-threatening situation (think chest pain, severe injuries, or difficulty breathing), **call 999**. This is the UK's emergency number, and it works for medical emergencies, police, and fire services (Department for Science, Innovation and Technology, et al., 2021). Ambulances are dispatched quickly, and emergency calls are free. While emergency treatment is covered for everyone, you may need to pay for follow-up care if you're not a UK resident.

- Got a sprain, a minor infection, or a cut that needs stitches? Head to an Urgent Treatment Centre (UTC), also known as a walk-in clinic. These are great for non-life-threatening issues when you need prompt attention. You can simply walk in—no appointment needed—and they're available in most towns and cities.

- If you're dealing with a persistent cough or mild illness, seeing a General Practitioner (GP) is your best bet. GPs are local doctors who can help with non-urgent medical issues. As a tourist, you can ask for a *temporary registration* at a local clinic. If you prefer quicker service, private GPs are also an option, though you'll likely need to pay upfront.

- Many minor health concerns can be handled at a pharmacy. Pharmacists in the UK are highly trained and can provide advice and over-the-counter medications for issues like colds, headaches, or mild allergic reactions. They can even help you decide if you need to see a doctor.

- For quick medical advice without visiting a facility, you can call **111** - this is the NHS non-emergency helpline. It's available 24/7, and trained advisors can help you decide what type of care you need and direct you to the right local services. They can even book you an appointment if needed.

- Prescriptions in the UK work differently than in the US. US prescriptions aren't valid in the UK - you'll need to see a UK doctor to get medication. Some medications that require prescriptions in the US are available over-the-counter in the UK (and vice versa), so check with a pharmacist.

- Travel Insurance Tips:

  - Your US Health insurance may not cover you when you travel abroad – check before you leave home and buy health travel insurance. It can be relatively inexpensive.

  - While emergency care is available to everyone, having travel insurance is strongly recommended, as you may need to pay for follow-up care.

  - Keep your insurance documents handy and know your policy number.

  - Some policies require you to contact them before seeking non-emergency treatment. Keep receipts for any medical expenses as you'll need these for insurance claims.

- Dental Emergencies:

  - For urgent dental problems, you can call 111 to find an emergency dentist

  - Emergency dental treatment usually isn't free, even at NHS dentists

  - Most tourist areas have private dental practices that accept walk-in emergencies

- Important to note:

  - Hospital visits work differently - there's no need to provide payment details upfront for emergency care

  - If you need regular medication, bring enough for your entire trip plus extra in case of delays

  - Keep a list of any allergies or medical conditions translated into

English if English isn't your first language

  ○ Most UK hospitals have translation services available if needed

NHS and Private Options

While the NHS is an excellent resource, it's not your only option. The UK has a wide range of private healthcare providers, which can be a good choice if you're looking for faster service or more personalized care. Private clinics are especially common in big cities like London, Manchester, and Birmingham, offering everything from routine check-ups to specialist consultations.

Key Differences

- **NHS:** Affordable (or free in emergencies), but you might face longer wait times for non-urgent care.
- **Private:** Quicker appointments and shorter wait times, but you'll need to pay for the service upfront unless your travel insurance covers it.

Travel tip: If you have travel insurance, check its policy to see if it covers private medical care in the UK. If it does, keep your insurance details handy—you may need to show proof of coverage. Also, many private clinics will ask for upfront payment, so keep a credit card handy if you opt for this route.

Pharmacies, Prescriptions, and Over-the-Counter Medications

Pharmacies in the UK are a lifesaver for travelers. Look out for stores like Boots, Superdrug, or local chemists, which are easy to spot with their green cross signs.

Here's what you need to know:

- **Over-the-counter medications:** Need paracetamol (similar to Tylenol), ibuprofen, or antihistamines? You can get these without a prescription. UK pharmacies also stock cold remedies, throat lozenges, and other essentials.
- **Prescriptions:** If you need a prescription filled, visit a pharmacy with

your UK doctor's note. NHS prescriptions are standard across the country (£9.65 per item in England, as of 2025), though they're free in Scotland, Wales, and Northern Ireland.

- **Ask the pharmacist:** Don't hesitate to ask for advice. Pharmacists are highly trained and can provide medical guidance for minor issues. If your symptoms require a doctor's attention, they'll let you know.

Emergency Numbers and Other Useful Assistance

It's always good to be prepared, so here's a quick reference list:

- For emergency medical help (life-threatening situations), call 999.
- For non-urgent medical advice (help deciding what to do or where to go), dial 111.
- For police or fire emergencies, dial 999 or 112 (the latter is the Europe-wide emergency number).
- For non-emergency police matters, such as reporting a lost item or minor theft, you can dial 101. It's a quick and straightforward way to get assistance without tying up the emergency lines.

Travel tip: Save these numbers in your phone so you don't have to scramble in case of an emergency.

Passport Help

If you lose your passport or need consular assistance, contact the US embassy in London or the nearest consulate. They can help issue emergency travel documents, provide guidance, and even assist in case of emergencies. Check the Appendix of this book for the phone number.

Pro tip: Make sure to keep a photocopy of your passport (or a digital version on your phone) as a backup—it will make replacing it much easier!

Smart Traveler Enrollment Program

To stay ahead of potential travel issues, consider enrolling in the Smart Traveler Enrollment Program (STEP). This free program, offered by the US State Department, keeps you updated on important safety and security information while you're abroad. (*Smart Traveler Enrollment Program*, 2025) By enrolling, you'll receive alerts about any local issues, such as strikes, natural disasters, or political events, that could affect your trip. Plus, it makes it easier for the nearest US embassy or consulate to reach you in case of an emergency. You can learn more about the program or sign up at the US State Department's official travel website.

Insurance Considerations

Travel insurance is your best friend when it comes to staying covered while abroad—it's better to have it and not need it than to need it and not have it! A good travel insurance policy can cover medical emergencies, but it's important to understand the specifics of your policy before you board your flight.

What to look for in travel insurance:

- Does it cover emergency medical care and hospital stays?
- Are private healthcare costs included?
- Does it cover emergency evacuation or repatriation?
- Will it reimburse you for prescription medication or doctor visits?

Important tip: Most US health insurance policies do not cover medical incidents that occur outside of North America. Before you leave home, take a close look at your current health insurance policy to check if you're covered abroad. If not, consider purchasing a separate travel medical insurance policy. These policies can be relatively inexpensive and could save you from significant financial stress in the event of a medical emergency.

Companies like Allianz or GeoBlue offer affordable options for short-term medical coverage during your trip. Policies like these can include coverage for emergency medical care, evacuation, and even repatriation if needed. Don't forget to shop around and read reviews to find a plan that suits your needs.

Travel tip: Keep a physical copy of your insurance policy and the emergency contact numbers handy during your trip. It's also a good idea to save a digital copy on your phone or in your email for easy access.

Travel Insurance and Healthcare Tips

Here are some additional tips to make your trip as smooth as possible:

Bring Enough Medication

If you take regular medication, pack enough to last your entire trip, plus a little extra in case of delays. Always keep your medication in your personal item bag to ensure it's easily accessible, or split it between your carry-on and personal item for added safety. Be sure to keep it in its original packaging and carry a copy of your prescription to avoid any issues at customs. This will help ensure you're prepared, no matter what surprises travel might throw your way!

Stay Hydrated and Well-Rested

Many health issues while traveling are due to dehydration or exhaustion. Carry a water bottle, take breaks, and pace yourself—especially if you're exploring cities on foot. Even in a developed country like the UK where tap water is generally safe to drink, it's best to stick to bottled water whenever possible for peace of mind, especially if you're sensitive to changes in water taste or treatment methods. Whatever you choose, staying hydrated is key to keeping your energy levels up and fully enjoying your adventures.

Use Sunscreen

Yes, even in the famously cloudy UK, you can get sunburned. Protect your skin, especially during the summer months.

Have a Mini First-Aid Kit

Pack essentials like adhesive bandages, painkillers, antiseptic cream, and any other basics you might need on the go.

HEALTH AND MEDICAL CARE

Know Your Coverage

Check what your travel insurance covers and carry proof of insurance with you.

While it's great to know what to do in case of illness, prevention is key! With this chapter in your back pocket, you'll be well-equipped to handle anything from minor sniffles to unexpected emergencies during your UK trip. The key is to stay informed, be prepared, and enjoy your adventure without worry.

Here's to a healthy, happy, and stress-free journey!

Chapter Thirteen

I Love It Here! Moving to the UK

So, you've fallen in love with the UK—its historic cobblestone streets, cozy tea shops, vibrant cities, rolling countryside, and the polite, queue-loving locals. Whatever your reason, you're thinking, *I don't want to leave—I want to live here!* But moving to the UK isn't as simple as packing your bags and hopping on a plane. Whether it's navigating visa requirements, finding a job, or adapting to British culture, there's a lot to plan and consider.

Don't worry, though—we'll walk you through everything you need to know to make your move as smooth and stress-free as possible. By the end of this chapter, you'll feel confident and ready to take on your British adventure!

Visa and Residency Requirements

The first and most important step to moving to the UK is understanding the visa and residency requirements. You can't just show up and stay indefinitely (as much as we'd all love to do that!). The UK has specific visa categories, and your eligibility depends on factors like your nationality, employment status, and long-term plans.

If you're planning to stay for a short period, such as for work or study, you'll need a *short-term visa*. For example, if you're studying at a UK university, you'll need a *student visa*, which covers the duration of your course plus a bit of extra time to settle in or pack up at the end. Temporary work visas, like the *Tier 5 visa*, are also available for certain schemes, such as internships or working holidays. These short-term visas each come with their own specific requirements and timeframes, so it's worth starting your application well in advance of your planned move. And here's a handy tip: while the visa application process might seem daunting at first, the UK government website offers detailed guidance and checklists for each visa type, making it much easier to ensure you've got all your documentation in order.

For those planning a longer-term move, the options get a bit more specific. *Family visas* allow you to join close relatives who are UK citizens or residents, while *innovator visas* or *investor visas* are designed for entrepreneurs or individuals planning to invest significantly in the UK economy. If you have specialized skills, such as in technology, the arts, medicine, or science, you might qualify for a *global talent visa*, which allows you to work and live in the UK without needing a job offer upfront. However, if you're coming for a job, a *skilled worker visa* (previously called the Tier 2 Visa) might be what you need, as long as you've secured a job offer with a UK employer who can sponsor your visa.

Once you've lived in the UK for several years (usually five, depending on your visa type), you may become eligible for Indefinite Leave to Remain (ILR). This status is similar to permanent residency and means you can live, work, and study in the UK without time restrictions. After holding ILR for 12 months, you can even apply for British citizenship if you meet the requirements.

Travel tip: The rules around visas can change, so always check the UK government's official website for the most up-to-date information before making any decisions. https://www.gov.uk/browse/visas-immigration

Citizenship by Descent

If you have a parent who was born in the UK, you might have a direct path to British citizenship that bypasses the usual visa requirements. This route is called "British citizenship by descent" and means you could be automatically considered a British citizen if you were born to a parent who was a UK citizen "not by descent" (meaning they were born or naturalized in the UK). However, it's important to note that this right typically only extends one generation - so if your parent was also a British citizen by descent (for example, if they got their citizenship through their own parent), you would not automatically qualify, though you might still have other options for claiming citizenship.

Many Americans are surprised to learn they might have a path to living in the UK through Irish citizenship. If you had a grandparent who was born in Ireland (or in some rare cases, even a great-grandparent), you may be eligible to claim Irish citizenship through Ireland's Foreign Birth Registration process. Once you've obtained your Irish citizenship and passport, you gain the right to live and work anywhere in Ireland or the UK thanks to the Common Travel Area agreement between Ireland and the UK, which continues even after Brexit. This route has become increasingly popular among Americans with Irish heritage, though it's worth noting that the application process can take several months to complete, and you'll need to gather substantial documentation to prove your Irish ancestry.

Finding a Job and Understanding UK Employment Culture

If you're planning to work in the UK, finding a job will be one of your priorities. The UK has a diverse job market with opportunities in many industries, but competition can be tough, especially in popular cities like London or Manchester. To start your job search, it's helpful to narrow down your focus to industries that are actively hiring. For example, fields like IT, healthcare, education, finance, and engineering often have a high demand for skilled workers.

Job-hunting in the UK usually begins online. Websites like Indeed, Reed, and LinkedIn are popular platforms where employers post job listings, and you can upload your CV to apply. Another option is to work with recruitment agencies, which can help match you with roles in your industry. Networking is also a valuable tool; attending career fairs, joining professional organizations, or connecting with industry professionals on LinkedIn can open up opportunities you might not find elsewhere.

Make sure to tailor your CV (resume) to match UK standards. British CVs tend to be detailed, with a focus on relevant skills and work experience, and should always be accompanied by a polite and customized cover letter. If you're applying for a job in a competitive industry, you may want to highlight transferable skills that make you stand out. Remember that British employers often look for evidence of cultural fit and adaptability, so don't be shy about mentioning any previous international experience or your enthusiasm for working in a British environment! One important note: British CVs typically don't include a photo or personal details like age or marital status - keep it professional and focused on your qualifications and achievements, and you'll be right on track with local expectations.

Understanding the UK salary structure and benefits system is crucial when job hunting. Unlike in the US, job listings in the UK often quote salaries as annual amounts before tax (displayed as "£XX,XXX p.a." or "per annum"), and many include benefits like pension contributions, private healthcare, and a set number of holiday days (typically 20-25 days plus bank holidays). It's also worth noting that some benefits Americans consider standard, like health insurance, work differently in the UK since healthcare is provided through the NHS. However, many employers still offer private health insurance as a supplementary benefit.

Moving via Graduate Studies

Moving to the UK for graduate studies can be an excellent pathway to experiencing British life while advancing your education. Most UK master's programs are notably shorter than their US counterparts - typically lasting just one year of intensive study rather than two or more years - which can mean lower overall costs despite the higher annual tuition fees. The process starts with securing admission to your chosen program, after which you'll need to apply for a Student visa (previously called Tier 4). The good news is that recent changes to UK immigration policy now allow graduate students to stay in the country for up to two years after completing their degree through the Graduate Route visa, giving you time to gain work experience or search for a permanent job without immediate employer sponsorship. Many universities also offer significant support for international students, from help with accommodation and banking to career services and cultural adaptation programs.

Renting or Buying Property in the UK

Housing is another important consideration when moving to the UK. Most people start by renting a home, as it's more flexible and requires less financial commitment than buying property. The rental market in the UK offers a wide variety of options, from city-center flats to countryside cottages.

To find a rental property, you can use popular websites like Rightmove, Zoopla, or SpareRoom, which cater to both full rentals and shared accommodations. Renting costs can vary significantly depending on where you live, with London being one of the most expensive cities in the world. In contrast, smaller towns and rural areas often offer more affordable options. Before signing a rental agreement, make sure to budget for a deposit (typically one month's rent) and possibly an agency fee, though this has been banned in some parts of the UK.

If you're planning to stay in the UK long-term and are ready to invest, buying property might be a good idea. The process involves finding a home, securing a mortgage, and working with a solicitor to handle the legal side of the transaction. House prices also vary widely across the UK, with homes in the South of England often costing more than those in the North or Scotland. Before committing to a purchase, take time to explore different areas and figure out where you feel most comfortable living.

Adapting to British Culture and Social Norms

Moving to a new country isn't just about logistics—it's also about adapting to a new way of life. The UK has a rich and unique culture, and understanding the basics of British etiquette and social norms will make your transition much smoother.

For starters, the British are famously polite, so phrases like "please," "thank you," and "sorry" are used frequently in everyday conversations. Queuing (standing in line) is almost a national pastime, and jumping the queue is considered very rude. Small talk is common, and you can almost always break the ice by commenting on the weather—it's a topic Brits never get tired of discussing!

It's also important to understand the basics of UK workplace culture, as it may differ from what you're used to. British workplaces are often formal but friendly, with an emphasis on politeness and professionalism. Punctuality is taken seriously, so always aim to arrive on time for meetings or appointments. Work-life balance is also valued, and most employees leave work on time and enjoy their evenings and weekends without interruption from emails or calls. If you're offered tea during a meeting or a quick "tea break" in the office, embrace it—it's part of British culture!

Cultural Adaptation and Community Resources

Moving to a new country can sometimes feel lonely, especially if you don't know anyone there. One of the best ways to feel at home is to build a community around yourself. Joining clubs, attending local events, or volunteering for a cause you're passionate about are all great ways to meet people and make new friends.

The UK also has a large expat community, and there are many resources available to help you connect with others who are in the same boat. Websites like Expat.com and Internations offer forums and events where you can meet fellow expats and share advice. Local community centers or libraries may also have groups or classes you can join, whether you're interested in learning a new skill or simply meeting new people.

Embarking on your UK adventure is nothing short of exhilarating! With a bit of careful planning and a dash of curiosity, you'll soon be navigating the visa maze, job hunting, house hunting, and finding your place in this vibrant country. So, whether you're dreaming of life in the bustling streets of London, the historic charm of Edinburgh, or the serene countryside of Cornwall, each step will be a chance to learn and grow.

So, pack your bags and get ready for a whirlwind of excitement—the UK is waiting to welcome you with open arms and a warm cup of tea!

Chapter Fourteen

Conclusion and Travel Tips

Congratulations! You've reached the final chapter of this guide, and by now, you're fully equipped to make the most of your trip to the UK. We've covered everything from planning and packing to navigating British culture, transportation, and health systems. This chapter won't repeat what we've already discussed, but will instead serve as a simple recap and final checklist to ensure you feel prepared and confident before you go.

Whether you're headed to the UK for a week, a month, or something longer, the goal is for you to enjoy your experience without stress. Let's wrap things up with a few last-minute tips, reminders, and useful advice.

Final Checklist Before You Travel

Here's a quick recap of essential tasks to complete before you head to the airport:

- **Documents:** Ensure your passport is valid for your entire trip (and ideally for six months after your return). If you need a visa, double-check that you have the right one for your stay. Keep both physical and digital copies of your travel documents, including your insurance policy, tickets, accommodation confirmations, and ID.

- **Health prep:** Pack any medications you regularly take, and ensure you bring them in their original packaging, along with a copy of your prescription. Get updated on vaccines. If you're concerned about unexpected medical costs, make sure your travel insurance includes comprehensive coverage for emergencies.

- **Finances:** Notify your bank of your travel dates to avoid any issues with your credit or debit cards while abroad. Carry a mix of cash and cards, and familiarize yourself with how to use contactless payments, as they're very popular in the UK.

- **Packing:** The UK's weather can be unpredictable, so pack for all seasons: layers, a waterproof jacket, and comfortable walking shoes are essential. Don't forget travel adapters for UK plug sockets and any electronics or chargers you'll need.

- **Itinerary and contacts:** Confirm your itinerary, accommodation details, and any transport arrangements. Save emergency contacts, including the UK emergency number (999), your travel insurance helpline, and your country's embassy or consulate information.

- Leave a copy of your itinerary and travel insurance information with your emergency contact back home.

Emergency Contacts and Resources

Hopefully, you won't need to use them, but it's always a good idea to have emergency numbers and resources handy:

- **Emergency services:** Dial 999 for urgent help (police, fire, ambulance, or coastguard).

- **Non-emergency medical help:** Call 111 for the NHS helpline, available 24/7.

- **Non-emergency police:** Dial 101 for reporting minor crimes or incidents.

- **Embassy/consulate:** The American Embassy in London is located at 33 Nine Elms Lane, London, SW11 7US. Keep contact details for your country's embassy or consulate in case of lost passports or other emergencies. Phone: +44 20 7499 9000

- **Travel insurance helpline:** Have your insurance provider's contact number easily accessible.

Having these details on hand can save valuable time and minimize stress if something unexpected happens.

Final Travel Tips

Finally, here are some last-minute pieces of advice to keep in mind as you embark on your UK adventure:

1. **Stay flexible:** Even the best plans can face hiccups, whether it's weather, transport delays, or unexpected closures. Be open to change and embrace the unexpected—it's all part of the journey!

2. **Blend in where you can:** While you'll always be a visitor, blending in with local customs and habits can intensify your experience. For example, avoid loud voices in public spaces, respect personal space, and take the time to appreciate the pace of British life.

3. **Make use of technology:** Download useful apps for maps, public transport, and local guides. Google Maps, Citymapper, and National Rail are great for navigation, while apps like TripAdvisor or Yelp can help you find restaurants and attractions.

4. **Stay safe online:** Use a VPN when connecting to public Wi-Fi networks to keep your personal information secure.

5. **Slow down and savor:** While it's tempting to cram every landmark and experience into one trip, give yourself time to enjoy each moment. Whether it's sipping tea in a cozy café, exploring a hidden alleyway, or soaking in the views of the countryside, the best memories often come from unplanned and unhurried moments.

6. **Skip the line on arriving home:** Before boarding your UK return flight, download the free Mobile Passport Control (MPC) app to breeze through US Customs like a seasoned traveler! This official CBP app lets you submit your passport and customs declaration information digitally before landing, then directs you to the (typically much shorter) MPC lanes upon arrival—potentially saving you hours of standing in those notoriously long entry queues after your transatlantic journey.

Enjoy the Adventure!

The UK is a truly special destination, filled with fascinating history, stunning landscapes, and warm, friendly people. Whether this is your first visit or the latest of many, you'll discover something new and memorable with every trip.

As you prepare to board your flight, remember that you've done the hard part—getting ready! Now it's time to enjoy every moment, from the big highlights to the small, unexpected surprises. Travel with an open mind, a curious spirit, and a sense of adventure.

Hopefully, this guide has given you the confidence and tools to make the most of your time in the UK. So go ahead, explore, discover, and make memories that will last a lifetime. Cheers to your adventure—you're going to love it here!

Safe and joyful travels!

Chapter Fifteen

Appendix

Information For Emergencies

Embassies

US Embassy in London

- 33 Nine Elms Lane, London, SW11 7US
- Phone: +44 20 7499 9000

Canadian Embassy in London

- Canada House, Trafalgar Square, London, SW1Y 5BJ
- Phone: +44 20 7004 6000

Emergency Contacts

Emergency Services (Police, Fire, Ambulance): Dial 999
Non-Emergency Police Assistance: Dial 101
General information and help with non-emergency health issues: Dial 111

Travel Services

Lost & Found (London Transport)

- Call +44 343 222 1234 or visit the Lost Property Office at Baker Street Station.

APPENDIX

National Rail Inquiries (Train Information)

- Call 03457 48 49 50 or visit www.nationalrail.co.uk for train schedules and updates.

Other Useful Contacts

Tourist Information Centre (London)

- Visit the London Tourist Information Centre at Leicester Square or call +44 20 7839 3483.

Quick Reference and Conversion Charts

Currency Conversions

- To get the most up-to-date rates, check with your bank or a currency exchange service, but here's a general guide:
  1 GBP = $1.25 USD
  1 GBP = $1.79 Canadian dollars
  1 Euro = $1.04 USD
  1 Euro = $1.49 Canadian dollars

Temperature Conversions

The UK uses Celsius for temperatures. To estimate: Multiply the Celsius temperature by 2, then add 30.

Distance Conversions

The UK uses miles for driving distances, but other measurements like kilometers are sometimes used in fitness or sports contexts.

1 mile = 1.6 kilometers
1 kilometer = 0.62 miles

Time Zone Differences

The UK is in the *Greenwich Mean Time (GMT)* zone, which shifts to *British Summer Time (BST)* during daylight saving time. However, the time changes happen on different days in the UK than the US, so double-check if you are traveling in late March or late October.

Basic Travel Tips

- Keep a physical paper copy of your travel insurance policy, passport, and emergency contacts.

- Consider buying a local SIM card or eSIM for cheaper data and calls.

- Download offline maps or a navigation app like Google Maps before heading out for the day.

- Public toilets are not always free, so carry some loose change with you (20–50p coins).

- Tap a contactless credit/debit card or an Oyster card to pay for public transportation—it's faster and cheaper than cash.

Health and Safety

- Stick to bottled water if you have a sensitive stomach or prefer an extra layer of caution.

- Pack any regular medication in your carry-on bag and bring a copy of your prescription.

- Stay hydrated and pace yourself, especially if walking or sightseeing for long hours.

This appendix serves as your ultimate reference tool during your UK adventure. Whether you're calculating distances, converting temperatures, or looking for a key address, this section is designed to give you the practical information you need, exactly when you need it. Enjoy your trip and make the most of your time in the UK!

Chapter Sixteen

References

American shop equivalents in the UK - target, pottery barn & more. (2024, March 4). ABroad Purpose. https://abroadpurpose.com/american-shop-equivalents-in-the-uk/

Arfin, F. (2024, October 31). *A guide to tipping in the United Kingdom.* TripSavvy. https://www.tripsavvy.com/when-is-tipping-expected-1662410

British money and currency (n.d.). Visit London. https://www.visitlondon.com/traveller-information/essential-information/money/british-money

Chang, J., Peysakhovich, F., Wang, W., & Zhu, J. (n.d.). *The UK health care system.* Columbia University School of Professional Studies.

Collins, T. (2024, July 24). *Transportation in the UK (Guide to how to get around).* UK Travel Planning. https://uktravelplanning.com/transportation-in-the-uk/

Collins, T. (2025, June 25). *Renting a car in the UK (practical guide & tips for visitors).* UK Travel Planning. https://uktravelplanning.com/renting-a-car-in-the-uk/

Cowie, J. (2017). Regional disparities in UK transport infrastructure. *Journal of Transport Geography, 63*, 120–130.

Department for Science, Innovation and Technology, Department of Health and Social Care, & Home Office. (2021, August 12). 999 and 112: the UK's national emergency numbers. GOV.UK. https://www.gov.uk/guidance/999-and-112-the-uks-national-emergency-numbers

Department for Transport. (2024, December 19). *Transport statistics Great Britain.* GOV.UK. https://www.gov.uk/government/collections/transport-statistics-great-britain

The drink drive limit. (n.d.). GOV.UK. https://www.gov.uk/drink-drive-limit

GO International. (2024, September 17). *Exploring the UK's thriving pub culture.* Gointernational.ca. https://gointernational.ca/exploring-the-uks-thriving-pub-culture/

Guide to buying a UK prepaid sim card in 2024. (2024, April 15). ESIM.net. https://www.esim.net/guides/buying-a-uk-prepaid-sim-card/

Home Office, UK Visas and Immigration, & Malhotra MP, S. (2024, November 27). *UK opens pre-travel requirement to non-Europeans.* GOV.UK. https://www.gov.uk/government/news/uk-opens-pre-travel-requirement-to-non-europeans

How to rent a car: What to know before renting a car. (n.d.). Avis.co.uk. https://www.avis.co.uk/drive-avis/car-hire-locations/europe/united-kingdom/airport-car-rental/know-before-you-go#

Kellner, P., & Thomas, W. H. (2025, January 7). *Traditional regions.* Encyclopedia Britannica. https://www.britannica.com/place/England/Traditional-regions

Mavromatakis, N. (2019). *Why do you have to place a hotel key card in a wall slot to operate the lights in a hotel room? What does it accomplish?* Quora. https://www.quora.com/Why-do-you-have-to-place-a-hotel-key-card-in-a-wall-slot-to-operate-the-lights-in-a-hotel-room-What-does-it-accomplish

Morris, A. (2023, June 28). *What is the minimum passport validity to enter the UK?* DavidsonMorris | Solicitors. https://www.davidsonmorris.com/what-is-the-minimum-passport-validity-to-enter-uk/

National railcards. (n.d.). NationalRail. https://www.nationalrail.co.uk/railcards/national-railcards/

Office for Health Improvement and Disparities. (2014, July 31). *NHS entitlements: Migrant health guide.* Gov.UK. https://www.gov.uk/guidance/nhs-entitlements-migrant-health-guide

Power plug & outlet Type G. (2024, December 27). World Standards. https://www.worldstandards.eu/electricity/plugs-and-sockets/g/

Processing times for US passports. (2024, October 3). Travel.state.gov. https://travel.state.gov/content/travel/en/passports/how-apply/processing-times.html

Reynolds, B. (2021). *How do British roads differ from American roads?* Quora. https://www.quora.com/How-do-British-roads-differ-from-American-roads

Royal mail and parcelforce worldwide UK services. (n.d.). Www.postoffice.co.uk. https://www.postoffice.co.uk/mail/uk-services

Searching for parking costs the UK £23.3 billion a year. (2017) Inrix. https://inrix.com/press-releases/parking-pain-uk/

Smart traveler enrollment program. (2025). MyTravelGov. https://mytravel.state.gov/s/step?gad_source=1&gclid=CjwKCAiAm-67BhBlEiwAEVftNqz0ea1WUP37iItzKsi85nOUt8X4BSwV9RRQCTnZZCINf1Saub1ELhoCOvYQAvD_BwE

Smith, R. (2020). Technological innovations in UK transportation apps. *Technology and Travel, 12*(5), 23–34.

Speed limits. (n.d.). GOV.UK. https://www.gov.uk/speed-limits

Svaiko, G. (2023, November 23). *Driving in the UK: A complete guide.* Wise. https://wise.com/gb/blog/driving-in-the-uk

Tax on shopping and services. (n.d.). GOV.UK. https://www.gov.uk/tax-on-shopping/taxfree-shopping

Tea Time: taste your tea according to the English tradition. (2021, May 20). Www.pages.fr. https://www.pages.fr/en/blog/post/tea-time-taste-your-tea-according-to-the english-tradition.html

The difference between the UK, Great Britain and the British Isles. (2011, August 3) Ordnance Survey. https://www.ordnancesurvey.co.uk/blog/whats-the-difference-between-uk-britain-and-british-isles

Worsnop, P. (2019). *What is the etiquette for tipping at restaurants or pubs in Great Britain and Ireland? Is tipping expected and common among locals?* Quora. https://www.quora.com/What-is-the-etiquette-for-tipping-at-restaurants-or-pubs-in-Great-Britain-and-Ireland-Is-tipping-expected-and-common-among-locals

Image References

Map of the British Isles – Extended Print License ID 106094443© Jktu21| Dreamstime.com

Map of the London Underground URL Code: https://content.tfl.gov.uk/standard-tube-map.pdf

British coins: ID 357319986 © John Hudson | Dreamstime.com

British paper currency ID 114045615 | British Notes © Hon Chung Ham | Dreamstime.com

Uk Electrical Plug Ianinhoose at English Wikipedia, Public domain, via Wikimedia Commons https://commons.wikimedia.org/wiki/File:Uk_13a_double_socket.jpg

SIM Card image Connorl9382, CC0, via Wikimedia Commons https://commons.wikimedia.org/wiki/File:Three_Replacement_SIM.jpg

Bed and Breakfast: ID 329794136 © Paul Gorvett | Dreamstime.com

Scone with Jam: ID 354643495 © Viktor Budyka | Dreamstime.com

Jacobite Steam Train: ID 112215511 | Uk Train © I L | Dreamstime.com

Paddington Station Board: ID 215422138 | Train © I Wei Huang | Dreamstime.com

British Train Ticket: ID 61156815 | British Train © John Williams | Dreamstime.com

www.ingramcontent.com/pod-product-compliance
Lightning Source LLC
Chambersburg PA
CBHW061809070526
44586CB00024B/2776